The Hospital Chaplain's Handbook

A guide for good practice

Mark Cobb

CANTERBURY
PRE
Norw

D1336127

First published in 2005 by the Canterbury Press Norwich
(a publishing imprint of Hymns Ancient & Modern Limited,
a registered charity)
St Mary's Works, St Mary's Plain,
Norwich, Norfolk, NR3 3BH

www.scm-canterburypress.co.uk

British Library Cataloguing in Publication data

A catalogue record for this book is available
from the British Library

ISBN 1-85311-477-4/9781-85311-477-9

Typeset by Regent Typesetting
Printed and bound in Great Britain by
William Clowes Ltd, Beccles, Suffolk

The Hospital Chaplain's Handbook

Contents

Foreword

Recently my colleague Harriet Mowat and I were commissioned by the Scottish Executive to carry out a research project which asked the question, *What do chaplains do?* We had the pleasure of spending 18 months with full-time chaplains in Scotland, exploring the nature, structure and practice of chaplaincy. We discovered many things about what chaplains do: their role in supporting staff, their careful and sensitive relationships with suffering people, their burgeoning management and administrative tasks and their ongoing task of raising the consciousness of healthcare professionals to the importance of spirituality for all aspects of healthcare. Diverse as the tasks of chaplaincy appeared to be, there was nevertheless a common underlying theme that implicitly and explicitly seemed to weld the various aspects together: chaplains *notice* dimensions of human experience that other professionals frequently do not. Their focus on the spiritual dimensions of human experience and the importance of this for patients and carers means that they view the task of healthcare from within a subtly different frame. This spiritual frame allows them to see dimensions of a patient's illness or a staff member's angst that are hidden from the professional gaze of others, not because of a lack of compassion or desire to care, but because they are simply not on the horizon of many healthcare professionals. Chaplains notice that which has, for various reasons, become 'invisible' within our systems of healthcare. Such a 'ministry of noticing' has significant implications for the shape and texture of the practices chaplains engage in. *But what is it that chaplains notice?*

One thing that is often overlooked within healthcare practices is the simple but crucial fact that illnesses *mean* different
things to different people. Cancer is not just a generic label
that can be applied in the same way to all people with a particular condition; it is a unique and transforming life event
that has deeply personal meaning for unique individuals.
Arthritis is not just the seizing up of body parts; it involves a
profound shift in self-image, personal identity and hopes and
possibilities for the future. Illnesses are deeply meaningful
events within people's lives, events that often challenge people
to think about their lives quite differently. Spirituality sits at
the heart of such experiences. A person's spirituality, whether
religious or non-religious, provides belief structures and ways
of coping through which people begin to rebuild and make
sense of their lives in times of trauma and distress. It offers
ways in which people can explain and cope with their illness
experiences and in so doing discover and maintain a sense
of hope, inner harmony and peacefulness in the midst of the
existential challenges illness inevitably brings. These experiences are not secondary to the 'real' process of clinical diagnosis and technical care. Rather they are crucial to the
complex dynamics of a person's movement towards health
and fullness of life even in the face of the most traumatic illness. It is this hidden spiritual dynamic that chaplains notice.
Enabling people to work with and care for this spiritual
dimension of their illness experience forms the heart of spiritual care and comprises the core of the task of the professional
chaplain.

In this important and impressive book, Mark Cobb offers
vital tools, perspectives and understandings that will enable
chaplains effectively to embark upon such a 'ministry of noticing'. It offers clear, sound practical guidance about what
chaplaincy is, what chaplains do and how chaplaincy can
(and should) be done within the NHS. Importantly the book
provides critical insights into spiritual care at both an interpersonal and an institutional level. Spiritual care is clearly
interpersonal, but the interpersonal aspects of spiritual care

are deeply impacted upon by the structural and institutional/
political aspects of the NHS. Cobb recognizes the significance
of this tension for chaplaincy and provides important insights,
structures and frameworks that will enable chaplains to both
understand and effectively navigate through the complexities
of providing spiritual care in the NHS.

The book is intended to be practical, and it most certainly
is. Nevertheless, it explores the practice of chaplaincy with a
theoretical and conceptual depth and clarity that roots and
grounds it in a way that draws out the importance of theory
for practice and the significance of practice for the construc-
tion of theory. Cobb is a true practical theologian! What
Mark Cobb presents in this book is important for all healthcare practitioners (not only chaplains). The book deserves to
be taken seriously and it is my hope and my prayer that those
who read it will be encouraged to notice things that they
perhaps did not notice before and in so doing move towards
developing the NHS as a service that is genuinely about *health*
and not just sickness.

John Swinton
University of Aberdeen

Acknowledgements

I would have found it impossible to write a book for and about hospital chaplaincy without drawing upon many experiences shared with others, countless discussions, and the many lessons learnt by working alongside other chaplains and other disciplines. This rich infusion has been an essential stimulus for what I have written and I am thankful to the patients, carers, colleagues and students from whom I have gained so much. Ideas for the book have been further developed through opportunities to speak at conferences, lead seminars and publish, all of which have enabled me to give form and substance to my thoughts and ideas.

My colleagues at Sheffield Teaching Hospitals have been an invaluable source of expertise and experience in hospital chaplaincy and the wider context of healthcare. Christine Smith and her colleagues at SCM-Canterbury Press have been patient and encouraging publishers. But my greatest appreciation is for Keith Arrowsmith, for being a willing and judicious reader of draft material and, more importantly, an unfailing support.

Finally, every effort has been made to trace and contact copyright holders, but if there have been any omissions these will be corrected in future editions. I am grateful to the following for permission to include material for which they hold the copyright:

'A Cradling Song', from *When Grief Is Raw* (Wild Goose Publications), words by John L. Bell and Graham Maule © 1987 WGRG, Iona Community, G2 3DH, Scotland.

A Gathering Prayer, from the Second Order for a Funeral Service, *Book of Common Order of the Church of Scotland* (1994), p. 264 © Panel of Worship of the Church of Scotland.

A prayer for those who mourn, reproduced with amendments in *Common Worship: Pastoral Services,* copyright material taken from *A New Zealand Prayer Book – He Karakia Mihinare o Aotearoa* (1989), p. 856 © The Anglican Church in Aotearoa, New Zealand and Polynesia.

'Christ our friend', 'God of intimacy', 'O God who brought us to birth' and 'A Prayer of Reconciliation', words and © Janet Morley, from *All Desires Known* (SPCK, 1992).

Common Worship: Services and Prayers for the Church of England and *Common Worship: Pastoral Services* © The Archbishops' Council 2000.

Confession and Absolution, Rite 2, from *An Anglican Prayer Book, 1989* © Provincial Trustees of the Church of the Province of Southern Africa.

'For you Jesus Christ came into the world', from *Uniting in Worship 2* © The Uniting Churches in Australia Assembly Commission on Liturgy (2005).

Health Care Chaplains Code of Conduct (2005) published by and © The Association of Hospice and Palliative Care Chaplains, The College of Health Care Chaplains and the Scottish Association of Chaplains in Healthcare.

'May God hold you as a lover', words and © Rosie Miles, from *A Book of Blessings*, Ruth Burgess (ed.) (Wild Goose Publications) www.ionabooks.com.

Prayers for the laying on of hands and anointing, words and © Jim Cotter, from *Healing – More or Less* (Cairns Publications, 1990), www.cottercairns.co.uk.

Introduction

In 1955, a small hardback book was published called *A Priest's Work in Hospital: A Handbook for Hospital Chaplains and Others of the Clergy Who Visit Hospitals*. The book was prepared by a committee that included a predecessor of mine at Sheffield, and the book aimed to provide 'a detailed picture of the varied and considerable work of a hospital chaplain'. The book contains a number of photographs that show chaplains ministering to the sick in hospital environments that are almost unrecognizable 50 years on. But despite the historical gap, the book's underpinning method remains valid, which is to understand the chaplain's role and function in relation to the context of healthcare. Understanding context is a key process in the pastoral cycle of practical theology, and it is a key task for any chaplain who is concerned about good practice. Therefore, like those who published in 1955, I will attend to a critical reading of context as much as I provide guidance and examples of good chaplaincy practice.

The context of healthcare is not self-contained and it is subject to larger environmental influences such as demographic and social trends, the politics and ideology of healthcare, and the discoveries of research. The picture of hospital chaplaincy is inevitably, therefore, one that is subject to being reframed – which in turn leads to the picture being redrawn or reinterpreted in order that it is still meaningful. Many of the recent discussions and debates within chaplaincy concern the boundaries of this frame, who sets them, and what their consequences are for the role and identity of chaplains. In 1955 it was the priest's work in hospital; 50 years on, it could equally be the work of an imam. In 1955 the concern was to demonstrate the relevance 'of religion to the healing art'; today the concern is about the relevance of spirituality. Despite this reframing and redrawing, the vitality of chaplaincy has never been greater. This is evident in the number of chaplains employed by the health service, the resources the NHS has committed to their development, the guidelines on chaplaincy published by the Department of Health, the activities of the professional associations, the number of published articles and chapters related to chaplaincy, and the few but significant studies about chaplaincy, including *Hospital Chaplaincy: Modern, Dependable?* by Helen Orchard (2000) and *What Do Chaplains Do? The Role of the Chaplain in Meeting the Spiritual Needs of Patients* by Harriet Mowat *et al.* (2005).

I have used the term 'chaplaincy department' throughout the text as this remains the most recognized terminology in the NHS and in the other national institutions that employ chaplains, such as the armed forces and the prison service. But there are alternative titles used that describe departments providing pastoral and spiritual care. Despite these titular variances, chaplains do similar work, share common intellectual and practical interests, have similar experiences and problems, and are likewise committed to caring for the ill and injured. These recognizable characteristics are how we identify people as chaplains and locate them on the social map, and this is what distinguishes chaplains from other disciplines, whatever title their departments use. Disciplines need boundaries to nurture and form practitioners, to focus on the development of particular skills and knowledge, and to articulate what is meant by good practice. There are, however, inherent tensions in this identity that derive first from the fact that most chaplains are also authoritative members of a faith community whose boundaries are not coterminous with healthcare, and second from the proposition that the spiritual dimension, to which chaplains' knowledge and skills relate, is not exclusive to chaplains. But far from being a problem, most chaplains hold this tension and use it creatively, enabling them to work across difficult boundaries and adding to the richness of the picture of chaplaincy.

This book begins (Chapter 1) by mapping out the context of the NHS both from a historical perspective and in terms of its contemporary structure, organization and workforce. It has been my intention throughout to reflect the current NHS context in which chaplains practise. Inevitably I have had to anticipate some developments, and others that were current when I wrote about them may now have been subject to revision or replacement. Readers should not therefore rely upon this text as a definitive statement, but refer to current guidance and policy.

Chapter 2 then focuses on what it means to be a chaplain, and although I have written this book for and about chaplains in general, it is inevitably influenced by, and evident of, my Anglican theology and ecclesiology. In Chapter 2 I also consider why being unwell may present a spiritual challenge for the individual as well as for a healthcare organization, and this becomes the basis from which I articulate the role of the chaplain. In order to fulfil this role, a chaplain needs to develop particular competencies and, along with other NHS staff, these are now identified within the NHS *Knowledge and Skills Framework* to which I refer. In addition, I address the question of how chaplains can develop their skills and knowledge and consider the importance of supervision.

Chaplains do not usually refer to themselves as clinicians, but the notion of clinical work is literally derived from bedside practice (Greek *klīnē*, meaning a bed). Chapter 3 is therefore about the clinical work of chaplains, which in most cases takes place at the bedside in wards and on units. The clinical environment is both a technical one and a social one and chaplains need to understand how to work in this environment effectively and safely. This requires knowledge of infection control procedures and how these relate to the tasks of a chaplain. Working in clinical areas also means understanding how clinical teams work and how chaplains can relate to them. The core clinical task for chaplains is spiritual care, and in Chapter 3 I explore the differences between the spiritual, religious and pastoral aspects of care. Chaplains, however, are a limited resource. Given also the large size of hospitals and the average length of stay, a means to identify patients with spiritual needs is required. I therefore discuss what it means to assess spiritual care needs using a framework approach and I also introduce the genogram and the ecomap as useful tools in exploring the wider context of the patient. Providing effective care to someone requires understanding something of this bigger picture, which also reminds chaplains that promoting the spiritual well-being of patients requires the addressing of factors beyond the individual that diminish humanity.

There are many specialist areas in which chaplains are expected to work and it is inevitable that these are experienced as disconnected and unrelated. I suggest in Chapter 4 that an alternative approach may be to consider spiritual care across the life-course along which people have to negotiate significant transitions from the cradle to the grave. The life-course approach sets the person within a continuous life-story or biography, but locates it within the particular nature of the transition. I illustrate this approach by considering four examples of transition from pregnancy and childbirth, mental health, critical care and older people. In each case I consider the spiritual and pastoral themes that may be present in the period of the life-course.

Chapter 5 is devoted entirely to the final transition, death – and in particular the impact of death on those who have been bereaved. Loss and bereavement are major themes in many of the contacts that chaplains have with people and in the rituals and services that they organize and conduct. I therefore explore the experience and expressions of grief from the basis of current research. Contrary to some views of bereavement, I consider that while it is painful and stressful, it is a normal reaction to death, and most people exhibit common patterns of grief in the early months following the death. I also suggest that one way that chaplains can support bereaved people is through listening to their stories of loss and helping them to narrate their experiences. Most support for bereaved people ends abruptly, and I therefore consider good practice in follow-up care and the type of support that is available to them in the wider community.

If we think of healthcare as a community then it reflects much of the diversity that is a feature of the UK in terms of different faiths, ethnicity and cultures. However, the defining characteristic of patients has often been their diagnosis, and I therefore consider in Chapter 6 how the concept of personal and group identity works in the healthcare context. I explore the relationship between self-identity and religious identity with reference to the Census of 2001 and I consider the challenges that this presents to chaplaincy. I suggest that chaplains from one faith tradition can engage with authenticity with those in need from other faith traditions and open up a space for caring dialogue and action. There is an increasing move for healthcare services to be provided with equity and in response to cultural differences. This is known as cultural competence, and I explore what it means for chaplains to develop the self-awareness, knowledge, skills and behaviour to enable them to respect the integrity of persons from different cultures and respond with sensitivity to the cultural dynamics of an encounter.

Chaplains rarely work in isolation and are usually members of a department. In Chapter 7, therefore, I consider what it means to be part of a well-functioning department that, if effective in fulfilling its tasks, is a rewarding and supportive place in which to work and has a distinctive and positive identity in the wider hospital. Many chaplaincy departments also run volunteer schemes that bring enormous benefits to the chaplains and patients while providing fulfilling and worthwhile opportunities to people wanting to participate in chaplaincy. I describe how a volunteer scheme can be implemented and suggest an outline volunteer role and person profile that clarifies expectations.

Chaplaincy departments also have to demonstrate that they

are delivering quality care, and so I apply the new *Standards for Better Health* to chaplaincy. This forms the basis for describing the audit process by which care can be systematically reviewed, and I give an example of a chaplaincy audit project that improves care. Finally, I consider the role of research in chaplaincy and argue that it can provide rigorous empirical knowledge that can inform pastoral action. Research begins with a question, and there are many questions about chaplaincy that could be developed into a research study. However, there remains a very limited research capacity in chaplaincy. I suggest therefore three levels of research activity, of which being aware of research is a level that all chaplains should be involved in.

Chaplains cannot exercise their role in any way they choose; there are ethical expectations placed upon them and limits to what they can do. These boundaries are explored in Chapter 8, in which I discuss the nature of ethical practice for chaplains and the inherent difficulties of caring relationships. A fundamental boundary in healthcare is that of confidentiality, but this has also become a contentious issue in relation to passing patient information to chaplains. I therefore explore the nature of confidentiality and the role of consent in the disclosure of information. Inevitably, this means discussing the Data Protection Act, on which I provide a critical reading. I also consider good practice in relationship to record-keeping. Most chaplains make notes on their contact with patients in some form or other, often as an *aide-mémoire*. I suggest that a more systematic approach to record-keeping can support good care practices and I outline the benefits of this type of documentation for chaplains.

A distinctive role of chaplains is in performing liturgical duties across a wide range of situations, from an individual patient to hospital event. In Chapter 9 I discuss the beneficial role of ritual and liturgy in healthcare and I suggest some principles of good practice. In the rest of the chapter I consider a number of situations in which liturgy and ritual will often play a role – for example, emergency baptism – and after discussing some of the issues about the particular situation, I then suggest some examples of good liturgy.

I have written this book to be a resource for chaplains and a critical reflection on chaplaincy in the context of today's health service. In my experience of teaching students and supervising new chaplains, there is frequently an expectation that there will be a textbook answer as to how to respond to a particular dilemma or complex situation. The manual of chaplaincy is a fantasy born out of anxiety. What I hope to have demonstrated is that by developing a habit of reflective practice and the rigour of practical theology, chaplains will have a firm grounding from which to make an informed response of compassion and care to those they encounter.

Mark Cobb
July 2005

I

The Context of the NHS

This introductory chapter to the NHS explains the context in which chaplains work. It outlines how health services and healthcare are structured, explains terminology, and provides a description of the major disciplines and professions that work in a hospital:

- Hospitals in history.
- The NHS today:
  - England
  - Scotland
  - Wales
  - Northern Ireland.
- Hospital structures.
- Foundation Trusts.
- Patient admissions to hospital.
- Staff in the NHS:
  - Nurses and midwives
  - Medical staff
  - The Allied Health Professions
  - Healthcare scientists.

Hospitals in history

Caring for the sick has always been a characteristic of Christianity, evident in the ministry of Jesus and the compassionate acts of individuals who sought to care for the ill in response to his command. As Christianity became established, organized and wealthy, the Church began to develop places of

care, initially for the stranger and traveller, and then for the
sick and impoverished. These medieval religious foundations
took varied forms such as hostels, infirmaries, almshouses,
asylums and hospices. They were generally small in size and
run by religious orders; therefore few survived the dissolution
of the monasteries in the sixteenth century and those that did
were re-established as secular and municipal institutions. An
example of this is the priory church and hospital of St
Bartholomew which was founded in 1123 by an Augustinian
monk. Henry VIII agreed to refound the hospital in 1546
following the closure of the priory church.

It was not until the eighteenth century that hospitals began
to be established whose descendants are still with us today.
While much medical practice still happened in the home
(when it could be afforded), surgery increasingly needed to be
housed in hospitals, and chronic illnesses required medical
wards. Voluntary hospitals were financed from historical
endowments, donations, fees and local authority grants.
Public or municipal hospitals sprang up in the nineteenth
century, providing infirmaries for the chronically sick as well
as institutions for the destitute. Funding came from local rates
and grants from government, and many began to develop into
acute units that matched or surpassed their voluntary neigh-
bours. The mental health sector remained independent, but in
comparison to the acute hospitals these institutions were often
large and set within extensive grounds. Psychiatry became a
specialized branch of medicine, along with the growth in the
institution of the asylum and its attendant physicians. The
specialist hospital also began at this time, usually in large
cities, and concentrated on a particular disease or system –
such as hospitals for women and eye hospitals.

Nursing was originally dominated by the religious orders,
but the discipline became increasingly secularized as it moved
to becoming an established profession towards the end of the
nineteenth century. Nursing schools became part of the hospital, but the religious disciplinary ethos continued, with the
retention of the title 'sister' and the prohibition on marriage

for student nurses. Doctors were trained through medical schools, most went on to become self-employed, and the profession was dominated by the privileged Royal Colleges and men – with women having to wait until 1876 for permission to qualify as doctors.

Healthcare was increasingly a public matter that became subject to more regulation and control. The epidemic diseases of industrial society led not only to social reform but also to a greater state responsibility, particularly for the 'sick poor'. Alongside these political and demographic changes, medicine was developing more reliable scientific knowledge and clinical treatments based upon research. Pharmacological and surgical advances enabled medicine to offer more benefits to society, to respond to disease and injury with greater effectiveness, and to raise people's expectations of its capability. Medicine therefore extended its role in society and came increasingly into the political arena as a necessary service to maintain the well-being of society. In 1939 the Ministry of Health took over the control of hospitals in order to cope with the casualties of war, and this financial and organizational necessity paved the way for the most extensive changes to health services ever seen in Britain.

The NHS in England and Wales was launched on 5 July 1948 and rationalized existing hospitals (municipal and voluntary), community services and GP services, following the ethos of the Welfare State and the pattern of the nationalized industries. The service aimed to be comprehensive in scope, available to all, and free at the point of delivery with its funding from taxation. This shift in healthcare came in a postwar period when food was still rationed, there was a housing crisis, and the British economy was on its knees. The creation of the NHS was less a revolutionary act and more the final and compromised realization of a solution to the inadequate provision of health services.

The nationalization of municipal and charitable hospitals brought them under government control within a regional framework that incorporated district and specialist services, medical and nursing schools. Hospitals were grouped together under a hospital management committee to provide a normal range of specialties. Local authorities had managed psychiatric hospitals and these now were grouped separately and had their own committee. Archbishop Fisher ensured that the Ministry of Health included chaplaincy as a core service and hospitals were advised to make appropriate appointments from the Roman Catholic, Anglican and Free Churches. This was an extension of the pastoral care offered by local clergy, but it was to become the basis upon which a distinctive NHS chaplaincy was to develop. To start with, there were approximately 28 full-time chaplains, mostly in teaching hospitals, initially employed by the new NHS. This number has grown continuously and it is currently estimated that there are over 400 full-time chaplains and 3,500 part-time chaplains employed by the NHS.

The NHS was established to combat one of the 'giants' that threatened society: disease. However, it was soon clear that this was not a finite task and the shortcomings of a government-funded service and the limits of medicine began to show. In addition to pressures upon public finance, the NHS has had to respond to endless innovation in medical technologies and therapies, increases in treatment rates, demographic and social changes. The pattern of service provision, though, remained unchanged until the introduction of competitive tendering for non-clinical services in the early 1980s and the division between purchaser and provider in 1990. Organizational changes have continued, and the present government has expressed its own aspirations in the White Paper *The New NHS*, from which has flowed more reforms for the ever-changing health service.

The NHS today

The UK Parliament is responsible for creating primary legislation, but it has recently moved to devolve certain powers to the individual countries of the UK in order that they can administer their own affairs. In particular, the provision of healthcare was substantially devolved following the creation of the Scottish Parliament, the Welsh Assembly and the Northern Ireland Assembly. Each country now has considerable autonomy to manage healthcare, allocate funding, configure services and determine policy. In England, the NHS is managed by the Department of Health which is implementing a new strategy (*The NHS Plan*) that aims to bring about far-reaching reforms to all aspects of care and the ways it is delivered. A patient-focus to services, disease-targeted clinical priorities, national quality standards and organizational changes are some of the principal aims of the strategy. The NHS is financed mainly through general taxation, with an element coming from National Insurance Contributions and the remainder from charges and receipts, including land sales and proceeds from income generation schemes. The planned expenditure on the NHS for 2005–06 is almost £73 billion. It is intended that 80 per cent of the NHS budget will be controlled by Primary Care Trusts.

England

The principal organizations in England for the delivery of services are the NHS Trusts (Figure 1) and these take three forms: first, Primary Care Trusts (PCTs) consist of large groups of GP practices and healthcare professionals who are responsible for providing primary health services and for commissioning the majority of secondary and community care services. Second, Care Trusts are NHS organizations that combine community health and social care services and carry out a range of other services, including social care, mental health services or primary care services. Third, NHS Trusts are responsible for most NHS hospitals and acute care. These various Trusts are accountable to a Strategic Health Authority (SHA) which ensures that the NHS organizations work together, creates a strategic framework for local health services, supports performance improvement, and manages the performance of

Figure 1   The NHS in England

Trusts in their areas. At a national level, chaplaincy is within the brief of the Chief Nursing Officer in the Department of Health, and the South Yorkshire Workforce Development Confederation has the national lead for developing the existing and future chaplaincy workforce.

Scotland

NHS Scotland is the responsibility of the Health Department of the Scottish Executive. There are both primary care and acute hospital self-governing Trusts in Scotland commissioned by area health boards. The Scottish Executive has set out plans for reform (*Partnership for Care*) that will bring about the abolition of Trusts in favour of local community health partnerships and unified NHS Boards. A Healthcare Chaplaincy Training and Development unit has been established to provide chaplains with training opportunities and to develop spiritual care policy and other initiatives.

Wales

The NHS in Wales is the responsibility of the National Assembly for Wales. There are 14 Trusts in Wales incorporating a range of community and hospital organizations, whose services are commissioned through 22 Local Health Boards (LHBs), which are coterminous with local authorities. A ten-year health programme (*Improving Health in Wales – A Plan for the NHS with its Partners*) sets out the strategic direction for healthcare in Wales.

Northern Ireland

The Department of Health, Social Services and Public Safety (DHSSPS) is responsible for health services in Northern Ireland. There are four Health and Social Service Boards in Northern Ireland, who commission services from 19 Trusts that include ten acute hospitals, community and social services. There are 15 Local Health and Social Care Groups (LHSCGs) based around GP practices that bring together providers of local primary and community services under a management board, and are responsible for the planning and delivery of primary and community care as well as contributing to commissioning decisions.

Hospital structures

The most common type of hospital is the District General Hospital (DGH), which offers a broad range of acute clinical specialities supported by diagnostic and therapeutic services such as pathology, radiology, physiotherapy and chaplaincy. Most DGHs have facilities for the emergency admission of patients either through an Accident and Emergency department, or as a direct referral from GPs, and provide day-case and outpatient services.

In addition, some hospitals provide specialist tertiary services and facilities at regional or national level. Hospitals that are linked to medical schools are referred to as teaching hospitals, although most hospitals offer learning opportunities for a wide variety of disciplines at a range of levels.

In England, the majority of services provided by hospitals are negotiated and commissioned through the PCTs, who receive an NHS income based upon a weighted capitation formula. One or more hospitals constitute an NHS Trust, which is a self-governing legal body responsible for providing acute care services. Hospitals are managed as part of the organization of a Trust through a board that comprises a chairperson, chief executive, executive and non-executive directors. The corporate strategic direction, key plans, performance monitoring and the fulfilment of statutory requirements are managed by the board. The board is corporately responsible for decisions and delegates its power through a managerial and organizational structure. The day-to-day management and leadership of the Trust is delegated to the chief executive who implements the Trust board's strategy and policies, oversees corporate and clinical governance, and ensures that the Trust operates in accordance with government policy. The chief executive is supported by the work of the other executive directors, who are responsible for such areas as finance, human resources, medical staff, nursing and estate management.

Hospitals require an organizational infrastructure to ensure the effective management and delivery of services (see Figure 2). Trusts have the freedom to organize themselves in ways that they consider make best use of their resources and deliver the services they are required to provide. Consequently, there

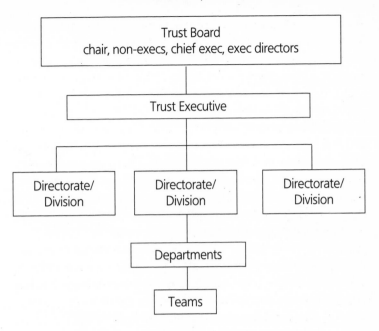

Figure 2　An example of a Trust structure

are a number of organizational models in use, but in most the management is divided at a number of levels and is within operational units such as the clinical specialties, support departments, directorates and groups. Management subdivisions have devolved responsibility for their own staff, budget, resources and strategic planning. A chaplaincy department fits within this structure: it is a discrete organizational unit with distinct aims and objectives; it requires financial and human resources, and a range of information from the organization; it needs to respond to certain needs within the organization; and it is held accountable for its performance. Chaplaincy departments are located in a range of places within hospitals, depending upon the size of the department and the management model of the hospital. Common locations include clinical directorates or divisions of Nursing or Allied Health Professions, Hotel Services and Human Resources.

Foundation Trusts

The strategic direction of the *NHS Plan* opened the way for greater devolution of power from the Department of Health to local services, and this has resulted in the development of NHS Foundation Trusts in England. These are legally independent organizations that operate within the NHS under licence from an independent regulator (Monitor), with a duty to provide NHS services to NHS patients. Foundation Trusts are intended to operate upon a social ownership model (e.g. co-operative societies), whose membership consists of local people, patients, carers and staff. Members can stand and vote in elections to the Trust's Board of Governors, who will represent the interests of the local community and partner organizations in the local health economy. NHS Foundation Trusts have much greater operational and financial freedoms, including the ability to raise finances for new facilities and to decide locally how to meet their obligations and priorities. But they are also required to maintain national standards for NHS services; treat patients according to need; and work in co-operation with other health and social care partners. The Healthcare Commission will assess the performance of Foundation Trusts, carry out independent reviews of complaints against them, and investigate serious failures in their services.

Patient admissions to hospital

Admissions to hospitals follow two basic routes: emergency and planned admissions. Emergency admissions result from either traumas that require immediate attention such as serious road traffic accidents, or medical emergencies such as a heart attack. Planned admissions result from people requiring medical attention or elective surgery that is not urgent, and can be dealt with as part of a hospital's routine work. This means that patients fall into two broad categories: those for whom an admission to hospital is unplanned and has been the result of a traumatic and unexpected event; and those for whom admission is planned and has been the result of a diagnosis requiring a non-urgent medical or surgical intervention.

Hospitals operate a variety of systems to control the admission of patients and ensure that tensions between supply and demand are managed. Some patients will need to go no further than an outpatients' clinic or a day-case unit. Emergency admissions, usually via ambulance, can involve triage and rapid assessment, whereas routine admissions come via waiting lists, and clinical priorities are used to regulate the flow of patients into hospital.

Most patients have been referred by a GP to a hospital consultant. Once admitted, they enter into a complex system of care involving diagnosis, medical treatment, surgery, rehabilitation and discharge. This patient care pathway involves a range of staff, constituting a multidisciplinary clinical team that is necessary to meet the patient's needs.

Staff in the NHS

The NHS employs over 1.3 million staff, represented by five major groups (Figure 3) and divided into over 70 disciplines. The major clinical professions and divisions are given in Table 1, and these demonstrate the specialisms within healthcare. Many of these will form the basis of a clinical department or grouping. The career pathways vary, but most incorporate a period of pre-clinical education, clinical training, post-qualification training and continuing development. Health professionals are typically subject to some form of state registration that ensures a uniform standard of competent practice and protects the public from unprofessional and unethical behaviour. Professional bodies regulate education and training, promote accountability, exercise disciplinary standards and maintain the public register of individuals fit to practise.

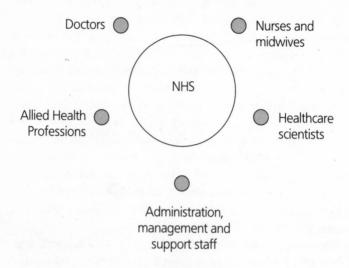

Figure 3   NHS staff groups

Nurses and midwives

Nurses, midwives and health visitors form the largest single group within the NHS and around 670,000 are currently registered. Nurses provide a wide range of care for the sick and injured. Midwives give supervision, care and advice to women during pregnancy, labour and the postpartum period. Health visitors are qualified nurses who promote health and well-being in the community. The Nursing and Midwives Council took over from the United Kingdom Central Council as the regulatory body, setting educational standards and dealing with complaints. Pre-registration education for nurses is in the form of a diploma of higher education or a degree course that consist of a common foundation programme followed by a programme in one of the four branches of nursing: adult, mental health, learning disabilities, or children's nursing. Around half of the programme is in the form of supervised nursing practice. Health visitors undertake

Doctors
- Accident and Emergency
- Audiology
- Cardiology
- Dental Surgery
- Dermatology
- Endocrinology
- Gastroenterology
- General (Internal Medicine)
- General Practice
- Genito-urinary Medicine
- Geriatric Medicine
- Haematology
- Immunology
- Infection and Tropical Medicine
- Intensive Care
- Medical Oncology and Radiotherapy
- Neurology
- Obstetrics and Gynaecology
- Occupational Medicine
- Ophthalmology
- Paediatrics
- Palliative Medicine
- Pathology
- Pharmaceutical Medicine
- Psychiatry
- Public Health Medicine
- Radiology
- Renal Medicine
- Respiratory Medicine
- Rheumatology and Rehabilitation
- Sports Medicine

Surgery
- Cardiothoracic
- General Surgery
- Neurosurgery
- Oral and Maxillofacial
- Otolaryngology
- Paediatric Surgery
- Plastic Surgery
- Trauma and Orthopaedic
- Urology

Nursing and Midwifery
- Adult Nursing
- Children's Nursing
- Health Visiting
- Learning Disability Nursing
- Mental Health Nursing
- Midwifery

Allied Health Professionals
- Art Therapy
- Chaplaincy
- Chiropody/Podiatry
- Dietetics
- Medical Social Work
- Occupational Therapy
- Orthoptics
- Paramedics
- Physiotherapy
- Prosthetics and Orthotics
- Psychology
- Psychotherapy
- Radiography
- Speech and Language Therapy

Table 1   NHS clinical professional groups and major specialities

Healthcare Scientists	• Medical Physics
• Biomedical Science	• Microbiology
• Clinical Physiology	• Pathology
• Engineering	• Pharmacy
• Medical Illustration	• Technology

Table 1   NHS clinical professional groups and major specialities (cont.)

additional post-registration training, usually a degree in health visiting. Midwives also follow a diploma or degree path with supervised practice. Continuing education is a necessary requirement of registration, and specialist awards and higher degrees are available. This forms part of the professional career pathway for nurses and midwives whose developing competencies are reflected in their graded titles. Senior roles now include Modern Matrons, who have overall charge of a group of hospital wards, and Nurse Consultants, who combine specialist practice with leadership, consultancy, education and research responsibilities.

Medical staff

Doctors remain the leading professional group within the NHS and there are currently about 200,000 doctors registered with the General Medical Council. Doctors are responsible for the diagnosis, care and treatment of illnesses and injuries, and can be divided into physicians, surgeons and general practitioners. Medical students usually undertake five years of university study and then undertake a two-year Foundation Programme of general training which leads to specialist/general practice training. The first year of the Foundation Programme allows provisionally registered doctors (Pre-Registration House Officers) to build upon the knowledge, skills and competencies acquired in their undergraduate training; gain new knowledge and skills; further develop their professional attitudes and behaviour; and show that they are practising in line with the principles of the medical professional in order to receive their full registration as Senior House Officers. The second year encompasses the generic competencies applicable to all areas of medicine, including team working, the use of evidence and data, time management, communication and IT skills, although the main focus of training will be the assessment and management of the acutely ill patient.

Once foundation training has been completed, doctors enter into specialist and general practice training. In addition, doctors can pursue career paths in public health, research and private practice. Post-registration training for hospital doctors is directed at specialization, with the aim of becoming a consultant. The Royal Colleges of Physicians, Surgeons and General Practitioners are independent professional bodies that supervise and provide training, administer examinations, award College membership and promote professional standards. Accredited continuing professional education programmes are provided by the Colleges and this forms the basis of a doctor's registration and revalidation.

The Allied Health Professions (AHPs)

This is a grouping covering a wide range of disciplines that provide clinical care and a range of outpatient and community services. There are currently 12 professional groups who are subject to state registration, and their standards of education, training, conduct and performance are overseen by the newly formed Health Professions Council. There are approximately 165,500 registrants: prosthetists and orthotists form the smallest group, with some 750 people; and physiotherapists the largest group, with around 39,500 people. Entry to each of the registered professions follows approved education and training, usually a diploma or degree course, as well as supervised practice. Post-registration training allows individuals to progress along a career path, and continuing professional development is usually necessary to maintain competence to practise through registration. There are other allied health professions who are not under the supervision of the Health Professions Council, and these include chaplains, clinical psychologists and medical social workers. However, chaplains, like many of their colleagues, retain some form of professional accountability through the authorization of their ministry by their faith group. An Anglican chaplain, for example, requires a licence issued by a diocesan bishop.

Healthcare scientists

This is a recently introduced generic grouping of scientific and technical staff that provides a diverse range of services. There are over 50,000 health scientists working in the NHS, in the fields of engineering and the physical, physiological and life sciences. Healthcare scientists work across the range of medical specialties and contribute to patient monitoring, testing, diagnosis, screening, treatment and research. In addition, disciplines within this group provide operational and technical support to clinical services. The diversity of this group is reflected in the range of educational entry levels, further or higher education courses, vocational training and professional programmes. Many but not all the disciplines within this group are subject to regulation or have access to higher specialist training and continuing professional development. Pharmacists are not strictly part of this grouping, but are associated with it through their scientifically based training and practice. There are around 40,000 registered pharmacists, most working in the community, with around 4,000 practising in NHS Trusts.

2

Being a Hospital Chaplain

This chapter begins by reflecting on the nature and vocation of ministry among the sick, as well as the close association of healing with wholeness. The spiritual impact of injury and illness is considered, and the need for healthcare to address the spiritual dimensions of a person. The role and responsibilities of a chaplain are outlined in relation to these tasks and the knowledge, skills and experience that underpin them. Finally, the ongoing formation of a chaplain is considered with suggestions for training, reflective practice, supervision and mentoring. This overview can be divided up into the following headings:

- Ministry and the care of the sick.
- The spiritual challenge of healthcare.
- The role of the hospital chaplain.
- Skills, knowledge and experience.
- Developing as a chaplain.

Ministry and the care of the sick

Helping people in need and looking after the sick is a moral characteristic of humanity. Human beings are vulnerable and variously dependent upon others for their well-being and continued existence. There is nothing exceptional about being ill; it is a common human experience, and individuals and communities respond in numerous ways to care for and support wounded humanity. Illness brings a loss of equilibrium to the well-being of the individual and it introduces inequalities into social relationships. Caring for the sick can therefore be considered a matter of social justice that protects and restores the critical interests and human needs of individuals and the integrity of society. This social and ethical perspective provides a rationale for the care of the sick that derives from a particular understanding of humankind and what we might mean when we talk of a 'good life' and a 'good society'. Christianity provides an additional perspective and tradition that also involves an understanding of what it means to be human and what it means to care.

The Christian tradition has an ancient heritage, a story rooted in sociocultural experiences, and a dynamic history in which the understanding and practice of care has changed and developed. The core theme that runs through this tradition has been the nature of the relationship between an individual, God and persons in need of care. This is a covenant relationship with the compassionate God who faithfully cares and who requires us to strengthen the weak, heal the sick, bind up the injured, bring back the strayed, seek out the lost, and do justice. In the person of Jesus, the Word is made flesh, and faithful divine love is embodied in a ministry that recognizes as righteous those who give food to the hungry and drink to the thirsty, who welcome the stranger, clothe the naked, care for the sick and visit those in prison.

This social relationship of care is an expression of Christian faith inasmuch as it is the activity of people who strive to follow the way of Christ. In loving self and neighbour, there is hope of realizing God's world of peace and justice in the midst of suffering, sin and death. This response in love embodies the transforming gospel of God's grace and contributes in word and deed to the struggle of the poor and oppressed for a just and loving society in which people may become whole human beings. This includes the need to respond with compassion and care to the diseases and traumas that diminish people and dislocate them from society. The care of the sick can therefore be understood as part of the continuing liberating work of God to foster human wholeness, restore well-being (salvation) and release people from whatever makes life less than human. This situates care in a sociopolitical context that encompasses more than the individual and recognizes that striving for human wholeness is also a human struggle, and not exclusively or primarily a Christian one.

The gospel is for humanity and it is conveyed through people constituting a community of faith who have developed ecclesial institutions. All Christian people are called to be ministers of the gospel, but the Christian community has also developed traditions to designate certain individuals to fulfil a variety of delegated functions integral to the life of the community. This is most explicitly expressed through ordination, but it can also be a characteristic of lay offices. While these authorized roles are not an exhaustive expression of ministry as a whole, they are representative of the faith community and they are a focus and articulation of its ministerial life. In addition, ordained ministry is a sacramental expression of the life of the Church, and the clergy are designated with the particular authority to exercise a sacramental ministry on behalf of the whole community.

If pastoral care is understood to be limited to the Christian community, then ministers of the gospel will be no more than chaplains of churches. However, in following the ministerial pattern of Christ, the Church is called beyond itself into the world to reach out to all people. The ministry of the Church is thus characterized both by its catholicity as well as its apostolicity: it is diverse in nature and it is sent out into the world. We find this reflected in the medieval notion of the hospital, which provided a resting place and hospitality for the stranger and the guest (Latin: *hospes*). It is also present in contemporary social ministries that, for example, provide care for the homeless. The care of the sick in relationship to the ministry of the Church is therefore a vocation to live the gospel in the world, to reach out to those in need, and to be concerned for the individual within a wider relational and social context.

Ministry in the context of healthcare is not exclusively

Figure 4   The three communities of chaplaincy

defined by its relationship to a faith community because chaplaincy is located within three principal communities: the faith community, the healthcare community, and the professional community (see Figure 4). The representation of a faith community by a chaplain is expressed in relationship to the healthcare and disciplinary communities, and with a critical sensitivity to the people who use the chaplaincy service.

Chaplains in healthcare share with others a commitment to promote well-being and to care for the ill and injured. This moral commitment is the bedrock of the healthcare community and enables vulnerable and suffering individuals to trust their health and lives to designated strangers who can work with them, or when necessary act on their behalf. The sick and suffering approach the healthcare community because they need assistance and help to restore an equilibrium in their lives that illness or injury has disrupted; and where this is not possible, to find relief from suffering and the assurance of continuing care. The community of healthcare is therefore a community of service that seeks to promote the common good of health and well-being, which is the profession – literally, the public declaration or promise – of most healthcare organizations and the disciplines that work within them. This is the ground of trust and the ethical basis for practices and interactions, which in other relationships we may consider immoral or illegal.

Finally, chaplains constitute a distinctive disciplinary community in the sense that they do similar work, share common intellectual and practical interests, and are committed to pursuing how pastoral and spiritual care can help people. Disciplines need boundaries within which to nurture and form practitioners, to focus on the development of particular skills and knowledge, and to promote good practice. The professional associations of chaplains provide these boundaries in support of their members and in order to identify those committed to their standards.

The spiritual challenge of healthcare

Being 'well' is a characteristic of life that enables people to engage in the activities of living, their relationships with others, and their life-projects. Well-being and health contribute to an equilibrium of life that is unobtrusive and remains largely hidden. Illness and injury threaten or disrupt this equilibrium and remind people of the fragile nature of human existence and the frail flesh in which we are embodied. But the challenge is not simply a physical, psychological or social one because being unwell impacts upon the person as a whole and this includes the spiritual dimension. Being unwell therefore raises questions about life and its intentions: questions of why people suffer, of what it means to exist in the world, of life's finitude and destiny.

The spiritual dimension refers to the beliefs, meanings and values by which people orientate and shape their lives towards that which is significant, purposeful and worthwhile. This can encompass both the inner world of the self and the outer world of a larger transcendent reality. Spirituality is therefore experienced and expressed in a wide variety of ways, both individually and collectively, of which religions are the most prominent and social forms. However, the religious perspective does not provide a normative spirituality for everyone, and people also adopt spiritual beliefs and practices to address their individual needs without any religious motivation or pursuit.

An unwell person is someone whose beliefs, meanings and values may be threatened, dislocated or disintegrated. Impaired physical or psychological functions, limitations to daily activities and restrictions to the way people are usually involved in life situations may all undermine the coherence of their worldview and the shape it gives to life. The resulting spiritual needs are an indivisible part of the whole person and therefore need to be an integral aspect of the healthcare provided. Enabling spiritual well-being therefore should be considered along with the treatment and interventions necessary for addressing a person's health problems. In addition, an awareness of the spiritual orientation of patients may be relevant to understanding their health condition, deciding care options and promoting their well-being and recovery.

The spiritual challenge is evident for patients, but it is also a challenge for healthcare organizations whose systems, processes and structures may hinder or neglect the spiritual dimension. The challenge is at the individual, clinical and organizational levels where it is expressed through the humanity of care, the extent to which patients and staff are treated as persons, the ethical sensitivity and connectedness of the organization and its cultural values and worldview. An individualistic model of spirituality is prevalent in healthcare, but this is only part of the picture and the challenge remains to view spirituality within a wider context and to understand its consequences.

People diminished or threatened by dysfunction or impairment confront those who care for them with two fundamental questions: what can be done about the problem and how should you behave towards me? A common response to the former practical question is to identify the disorder as the object of enquiry and to follow a dispassionate course of analysis and problem-solving. The latter question concerns a task of quite a different nature: the identity and meaning of people who face disruption and uncertainty as a result of a health dilemma. This requires looking beyond the pathology to the person as a whole, and with compassion and commitment attending to the world of meaning. It is in this space that we may discern the spiritual dimensions of care.

The role of the hospital chaplain

Since the advent of the NHS in 1948 the primary role of chaplains has been widely accepted as meeting the spiritual needs of patients, carers, staff and students. The latest guidelines from the Department of Health reinforce that meeting these varied spiritual needs is fundamental to the care that the NHS provides. It is obvious from the outset that hospital chaplains are ministers to organizations and those who constitute them. This scope gives chaplains a unique position in a hospital, but it may also make it difficult for others to understand and locate the role. If chaplains serve both organizations and the individuals involved in them – whether as users or providers – then there is likely to be ambiguity. Chaplains also deal with the less tangible aspects of healthcare through stories, narratives and dialogues, both of individuals and communities: precious stories of hope, spoken and unspoken narratives of suffering, and dialogues exploring what we might mean by health, life and death. But for the chaplain this is more than a conversation, it is more than skill in communication, it is more than a competency in care, for it is the way we struggle to remember and find our identity as human beings. And it is in this search for meaning that the chaplain is a reminder of the spiritual dimension.

Remembering is essential to caring; in caring we have regard for another individual, we have to be attentive to the other. Therefore an important way of understanding the vocation of the chaplain is witnessing to the 'other', both in individuals and in organizations. This is an ethical and skilled practice that challenges the alienation and isolation of illness (the making of strangers), affirms humanity and nurtures hope. It is also a vicarious role in healthcare organizations, sustaining a memory of the spiritual, both symbolically and practically on behalf of others, some of whom may never explicitly acknowledge its significance or value.

How the role of a chaplain will be practically expressed will be determined to a large extent by the type of healthcare organization, the nature of its services, and the aims of the chaplaincy department. In addition, a chaplain's knowledge, skills, beliefs and faith tradition will shape the individual's practice of chaplaincy. Within the scope of practice, the role of the chaplain can be outlined in ten generic key tasks:

1 *Provide spiritual care and meet religious needs.* This principal task often derives from the needs of individuals, but may involve a wider network of carers and staff.
2 *Devise and conduct religious ceremonies and human rituals.* This may range from maintaining the requirements of religious observance to providing meaningful liturgy and the articulation of the sacred in the life-events of individuals or the healthcare community.
3 *Contribute to multidisciplinary teams.* Care that is co-ordinated around the diverse needs of the patient requires professionals to collaborate effectively, and this includes the participation of a chaplain.
4 *Provide bereavement care.* Most people end their life in hospital and carers often require supportive care in order to face the death of those significant to them and to deal with its consequences, including planning the funeral.
5 *Supervise chaplaincy volunteers and students on placement.* Chaplaincy departments often provide opportunities for volunteers and students training for ministry who require supervision and support.

6 *Participate in education and training.* Chaplains have specialist skills and knowledge that can be used to provide learning opportunities for other health professionals or members of faith communities.

7 *Contribute to organizational development.* The wide scope of the chaplains' role and their insight into organizational behaviour means that they can make effective contributions to problem-solving and provide a critical perspective on organizational ethics, values and beliefs.

8 *Participate in clinical audit, service review and research activity.* Chaplains should be involved in a range of activities to support best practice in order to maintain high standards, ensure that needs are being met and understand better what good spiritual care means.

9 *Contribute to service development.* The changing demands and context of healthcare require services to be responsive to needs and to plan ahead to ensure effective development.

10 *Liaise with local faith communities and voluntary groups.* Chaplains provide a link with the wider community that can facilitate the input of a more diverse range of faiths and bring an important user perspective and involvement into a healthcare organization.

Each of these tasks represents an interrelated aspect of chaplaincy and demonstrates the multidimensional nature of the chaplain's role. Different models of chaplaincy will put emphasis on particular tasks, and some usually have priority over others – in particular, responding to referrals of patients and carers may be considered core tasks. Tensions may therefore exist between the tasks and they may compete for time and resources. It is necessary that chaplains have a clear understanding of their own particular work areas and responsibilities and how these relate to both the overall priorities of the chaplaincy service and the requirements of the organization.

Skills, knowledge and experience

In order to function effectively in their role, chaplains need to be competent in a range of knowledge and skills. The context of healthcare means that some of these will be common to all healthcare practitioners – for example, communication skills – and some will be unique knowledge and skills specific to chaplains – for example, pastoral and spiritual care. Chaplaincy therefore constitutes a unique discipline because chaplains learn and practise a distinctive body of knowledge. This knowledge draws upon and integrates well-established theories, concepts and practice developed across a range of academic subjects, including theology and religious studies, psychology, the social sciences and the medical humanities including bioethics. In addition, chaplaincy knowledge can benefit from a basic understanding of relevant aspects of the clinical sciences including an understanding of common medical terminology, major disease processes, diagnostic investigations, common types of therapy and patient management.

The majority of people entering chaplaincy have undertaken prior learning and training in order to exercise ministry in a community setting. This will provide the basis from which to develop some of the competencies of a hospital chaplain and a baseline to assess their development needs. The NHS *Knowledge and Skills Framework* (KSF) is designed to identify the knowledge and skills that individuals need to apply in their posts and to guide their development, to which pay progression is related. The *KSF* defines 30 components or dimensions, of which six core dimensions apply to all jobs, and 24 specific dimensions relate to some jobs. Each dimension consists of a number of progressive levels representing advancing levels of knowledge and skill, as well as the increasing complexity of its application. The *KSF* is a generic tool and there will be variation in its application, but set out below are the core dimensions that will relate to all chaplains and the additional dimensions that will usually apply to a range of chaplaincy jobs:

Core dimensions

1 Effective communication with individuals and groups.
2 Development of skills and knowledge of self and contributing to the development of others.
3 Maintaining the health, safety and security of self and others.
4 Contributing to the development and improvement of services.
5 Maintaining and improving quality in all areas of work and practice.
6 Supporting the equality and valuing the diversity of people.

Specific dimensions (which relate to some but not all jobs)

HWB2	Assessment and care planning to meet people's spiritual health and well-being needs.
HWB4	Enabling people to meet their spiritual needs and empowering them to realize their potential.
HWB5	Planning, delivering and evaluating care to meet spiritual needs.
HWB6	Assessment of psychological functioning and treatment planning.
HWB7	Interventions and treatments to address psychological needs.
G1	Enabling people to learn and develop through structured approaches and programmes.
G2	Contributing to the development of new models and practices in chaplaincy.
G5	Managing services and projects.
G6	Managing individuals and teams.
G7	Developing the capacity and capability in the organization and workforce.
G8	Marketing and managing public relations for the chaplaincy service.

Source: Department of Health, *Knowledge and Skills Framework* (2004).

The competencies associated with these dimensions enable a chaplain to make the judgements and decisions necessary to contribute beneficially and safely to the healthcare of individuals and groups, to participate effectively in the healthcare organization and wider community, and to continue to develop and contextualize knowledge, understanding and skills.

Developing as a chaplain

Healthcare organizations offer a wide range of learning opportunities at different levels that are accessible to chaplains. Academic courses are available through many higher education institutions, and a number of chaplaincy organizations also provide and commission training. The progression of a chaplain from novice to expert level benefits from a structured approach that builds progressively upon learning and experience and may include the development of particular specialities such as care of the elderly or palliative care. The aspirations and interests of individual chaplains will be one of the important factors contributing to development, but account must also be taken of the particular demands of a chaplain's role and the needs of the healthcare organization. Chaplains must be able to demonstrate their ability to apply their knowledge and skills to meet the demands of their current post and they need to agree a personal development plan to achieve this aim with their line manager as well as plan for any career progression. It is good practice that chaplains undertake an annual review at which learning can be evaluated, development needs identified and a plan agreed to achieve their aims.

Important aspects of competent chaplaincy practice cannot be represented in propositional or conceptual form, but must be developed through professional formation. Practical knowledge of chaplaincy begins and is developed out of experience where theory and technique are given a human face that must be responsive to ambiguous and complex human situations. However, the subjective nature of this knowledge requires that it is placed in critical dialogue with the theory, practice and experience of chaplaincy and understood in relationship to self-awareness and self-knowledge. This self-conscious discipline is known as reflective practice and it can be defined as a deliberate process of critically interpreting and understanding experience through an active engagement with what we know of others, the particular context and ourselves. This inevitably requires a high degree of self-examination; the ability to be self-critical; an accurate empathy for others; and the ability to perceive what is unspoken or implicit in a situation. For these reasons it is accepted that regular supervision should be an essential requirement to support competent practice and ongoing development.

Supervision at its simplest is an intentional facilitated opportunity to reflect upon experience. This is important for chaplains because caring or helping relationships are always more complicated than they may appear for they contain ambiguity, inequality and an interpersonal dynamic that is beyond immediate introspection. The supervision session should be a place of honest reflection in which chaplains can explore openly their encounters with others and examine their motives, fears, barriers, blind spots and their own needs. Chaplains often care for others in ways that require intense involvement in emotionally challenging and distressing situations that contain high expectations. Stress and other psychological pressures are absorbed by chaplains, and supervision can be one way of discharging these in the process of monitoring and understanding stressors and the way we respond to them.

Chaplains are trusted to act in the best interests of those they care for and because this requires accommodating particular circumstances and human individuality they must have discretion to act within certain boundaries. Consequently, chaplains have an ethical responsibility to ensure that they exercise sound professional practice based upon good knowledge, understanding and experience. In supervision, chaplains have the opportunity to discuss with another practitioner the competency of their work, the unconsidered perspectives and interpretations, and the alternative approaches that could be taken. Supervision can therefore provide both a supportive and educative function, but whatever form it takes it is good practice that it is underpinned by an explicit agreement that articulates the aims and format of the sessions, the boundaries operated (including confidentiality) and the accountability of the supervisor.

Finally, it is recognized that all who work in the demanding and dynamic context of healthcare will benefit from new learning and the opportunity to develop practice. This is generally referred to as continuing professional development (CPD) and it refers to a wide range of learning activities that enable chaplains to maintain and enhance their knowledge, skills and understanding in the context of professional practice. It is a requirement of many healthcare professions that competent practice is demonstrated in part through CPD and it is expected that the professional associations of chaplaincy will recommend minimal levels of CPD activity for chaplains.

There are three basic categories of CPD:

1 **Individual activities**
    This is learning undertaken and evaluated by the chaplain without reference to other chaplains or external bodies. Examples include reading relevant journals and textbooks, structured reflective practice, presentations, participating in working parties, undertaking research, writing articles, chapters and books.

2 **Internal activities**
    This is activity that takes place within the health service and among healthcare professionals in which the chaplain participates with colleagues in local learning events and meetings. Examples include participating in in-house seminars, workshops, journal clubs, audit meetings, multi-disciplinary case reviews and regional professional meetings.

3 **External activities**

These are events usually provided by external bodies such as Higher Education Institutions, professional associations or commercial conference organizers on a regional, national or international context. Examples include attending conferences and obtaining recognized academic qualifications.

3

Clinical Work

Work in clinical areas is the primary task of chaplains and this chapter forms the core of the book. From the basics of how to behave on a ward through to self-care, this chapter considers the major aspects that a chaplain must address in clinical work.

- Ward etiquette.
- Infection control – handwashing and protective clothing.
- Multidisciplinary care.
- Spiritual, religious and pastoral care.
- Assessing spiritual care needs.
- Caring for the person in context.

Ward etiquette

The traditional place in which patients are collectively cared for is the ward. This clinical area is a place where the ill and injured can be watched over, protected and offered care and treatment. Historically, Nightingale Wards achieved this by using an open dormitory layout of beds in long rows, but most standard wards today are a combination of bays (in which there are usually four to six beds) and single-occupancy rooms. Wards constitute an organizational unit of care and they follow certain conventions, policies and protocols to ensure an efficient, safe and orderly environment for patients, their visitors and staff. It is therefore important that chaplains understand what is expected of them when they are on a ward, or in a clinical area, in terms of their behaviour and practice.

Ward etiquette is established through written policy and the personal attitudes of influential staff, all of which can create a distinctive ward 'ethos'. A chaplain will usually work on many different wards and needs to observe generic conventions as well as be sensitive to the particular ethos of individual clinical areas.

At its simplest, ward etiquette is about courtesy, good communication and safe practice (see Table 2). In reality, etiquette also relates to the social behaviour of a ward and the way it functions as a group. One of the most important elements of etiquette is derived from the hierarchical systems that pervade healthcare institutions. Hierarchies establish the level and scope of authority that individuals can exercise and therefore identify who is responsible for what. An explicit manifestation of hierarchy is the designation of an individual in terms of their grade. A ward is managed by a senior nurse who is responsible for all aspects of nursing and who, with nursing colleagues, co-ordinates the health and social care needs of patients. The senior nurse is the arbiter of many decisions about the day-to-day operations of a ward, and can be a key member of staff for a chaplain to liaise with.

It is a courtesy to make known your arrival on a ward at the nurses' station. This gives you the opportunity to make contact with nursing staff and to find out what is happening on the ward at that time (for example, there might be a ward round taking place). If you have come to the ward in response to the referral or follow-up of specific patients or carers, then these cases can be discussed with relevant nursing staff. If you are carrying out a general ward round then you can ask if staff are aware of anyone who might value chaplaincy contact. It is important before you have patient or carer contact to know of any relevant risk factors involved so that you can assess the situation and take adequate precautions (see Infection Control pp. 36–8 and Table 3). In particular, if you intend to administer any sacraments, then discuss this with a relevant health professional involved with the patient.

For example, you receive a referral for a patient who has

Security	• wear identification badges • know emergency numbers
Duty of confidentiality	• information about patients and their circumstances • patient's visitors • staff • hospital and Trust
Privacy and dignity	• respect for patients at all times • don't go behind curtains unless permission given • toilets/bathrooms are out of bounds
Awareness of patient's condition	• drowsy or tired • communication difficulties • hearing or sight impaired • acute symptoms (e.g. pain or nausea) • confused or disorientated
Do not move patients	• seek assistance from staff
Sitting near patients	• be aware of drips, catheters, drains and equipment – if in doubt, ask
Infection control	• handwashing • follow specific instructions (e.g. barrier nursing)
Emergency	• know what to do and how to get assistance if someone faints, has a seizure, or a respiratory or cardiac arrest

Table 2　Ward etiquette

recently been admitted following a stroke. In addition, you receive a phone call from the patient's vicar who informs you that the patient is a regular communicant. You identify that the patient's swallow may have been compromised as a result

---

Five steps of risk assessment

1 Identify the hazards that present a risk to patient health and safety or to your ability to manage and care for patients.
2 Consider the nature and scope of the hazard, the likelihood of it occurring, and its consequences.
3 Decide on the significance of the risk and whether to take action.
4 Implement measures to reduce or eliminate the risk.
5 Review the risk assessment.

Common risks
- Compromised immunity.
- Compromised skin integrity.
- Poor swallow function (dysphagia).
- Blood, body fluids, secretions and excretions.
- Behaviour that is aggressive or violent.
- Lone working.

Table 3   Risk assessment

---

of the stroke. The patient's speech and language therapist tells you that the patient has dysphagia and is currently unable to take any food or fluids by mouth. You decide with the advice of the therapist that at this stage there is a high risk of aspiration if the patient receives Holy Communion. You explain to the patient why you are unable to offer them Holy Communion, but that you will pray with them and you also offer to anoint them. You then follow up the patient and find out from the speech and language therapist whether the patient's swallowing reflex has improved.

Curtains are used around beds when people want privacy and you should never go behind curtains unless you have the express permission of the patient, carer or nurse. Remember that curtains only provide visual protection and offer no aural privacy. Never seek out patients in bathrooms or toilets. Always approach patients as persons and respect their personal space. Introduce yourself, give your name, tell the patient why you are there, and get their permission to continue the contact. It is perhaps a unique contribution of the chaplain to offer the patient the opportunity to decline chaplaincy contact. A patient who is being attended by another health professional should not in general be interrupted unless there is a more pressing need for the patient to be seen by a chaplain. In this case you should explain your need to attend the patient and the time you will need. Equally, you should not expect to be uninterrupted and ask other healthcare workers to wait until you have finished, unless the matter is more urgent.

There are times when clinical work is difficult to undertake because of the ward routine. This can include mealtimes, rest periods, assisted bathing and medical ward rounds. Visiting hours are for visitors, and not hospital chaplains, but they are the period when the social activity of a ward is at its highest. Some patients prefer to have time alone with those who have come to see them, others welcome the support of a chaplain; therefore each case needs to be sensitively assessed on an individual basis. In addition, patients are taken off the ward for diagnostic investigations, assessments, therapy and surgery. This is planned activity, but it does not necessarily occur when it has been scheduled and you should liaise with a relevant nurse if you need to see a patient at a particular time.

Infection control – handwashing and protective clothing

Healthcare practitioners are a major route of infection for patients, so chaplains must maintain high standards of hygiene in clinical practice. The primary measure that chaplains must take is observing the principles of hand hygiene in order to minimize the transmission of micro-organisms from patients and the environment to other patients. Hands should be washed before and after every episode of care involving direct contact with a patient's skin, food, invasive devices or dressings. It is difficult to predict or control what may happen during an encounter with a patient. You may pass a cup of water, reach out to hold a patient's hand, and make contact with a dressing or a cannula. You may be with a patient for the purpose of administering a Holy Communion wafer or anointing. A simple routine to follow therefore is to always wash your hands before you see a patient, and to wash them afterwards when this is required.

It is good practice to remove any hand jewellery before handwashing and you should cover any cuts and abrasions with a waterproof dressing. Plain soap and water used with a thorough washing technique is considered an effective means of making hands clean and decontaminating them to a level sufficient for the contact a chaplain may usually have with a patient. Wet your hands and apply the liquid soap, ensuring it comes into contact with all of the hand's surfaces. Rub together your hands vigorously and make sure you pay attention to your fingertips, thumbs and the areas between your fingers. Finally, rinse your hands thoroughly and dry them on paper towels. Where hands are not soiled an alcohol-based rub is an alternative to handwashing.

Gloves, aprons and masks are used to reduce the transmission of micro-organisms to patients and to protect staff from contamination by exposure to patients' body fluids, secretions and excretions. Use of protective clothing is decided on the basis of a risk assessment that will be carried out by nursing staff or members of the infection control team. One of the most common types of infection control routines is the use of barrier nursing, which requires staff to wear protective clothing when with the patient. Chaplains must follow instructions about infection control operating in a clinical area or for an individual patient. If you have doubt about infection control procedures, ask at the nursing station. You should discard any protective equipment you have used in the bins provided after each activity and wash your hands.

Infection control precautions can present practical difficulties for some aspects of pastoral care and they need to be considered before visiting a patient. The primary aim is to prevent the transmission of potential pathogens, and therefore in addition to hand hygiene the use of equipment, books and leaflets must be assessed when it is anticipated that they will come into contact with a patient. Communion sets should be avoided, and where they are used they should be decontaminated between each administration. The use of a pyx should avoid the difficulty of direct patient contact, but care still needs to be taken when administering a wafer directly on to a patient's tongue. It is also good practice to leave leaflets and service sheets with patients who are being barrier nursed.

Patients who are considered infectious or whose immunity is sufficiently compromised will not usually be allowed to attend a communal service in a chapel. For those patients who do attend a service, the risk of acquiring some infection is the usual one present in any group of people. However, leakage from urinary catheters or a patient vomiting is a situation that should be anticipated and a chapel should have the necessary supplies to contain such an event. No episode of disease has been attributed to sharing a common communion chalice, and there has been no research into this matter, but some consider that intinction may be a reasonable precautionary practice.

Multidisciplinary care

Teams exist in healthcare for two practical reasons: first, to ensure that care can be delivered effectively and consistently beyond the limits of an individual; second, to bring together the range of disciplines necessary to meet the needs of a patient. There are many forms and variations of teams, some are geographically based and others are constituted as working groups, which form a nucleus of staff. A ward or unit, for example, will typically have its own nursing team, alongside of which will operate medical, therapy and social work teams. Specialist areas, such as palliative care, may operate multi-disciplinary teams established around the needs of particular patient groups that draw upon a set of expertise to contribute to an integrated approach to care.

A clinical team comprises the staff who care for specified

groups of patients. It is based around staff who work on a particular ward, outpatient clinic, theatre suite or other location in a hospital, but also extends to other staff who care for the patient. A clinical team caring for patients who, for example, have a fractured neck of their femur might be based around the staff on an orthopaedic ward. Other staff who work in the Accident and Emergency department, theatres, rehabilitation, pharmacy, diagnostic units and the outpatients department have an input into the care of the patient and may also be included in the clinical team.

Teamwork is considered to be of great benefit to healthcare in terms of the quality and coherence of care they deliver, the consequent enhanced patient or user satisfaction, and the improved staff motivation, innovation, mental health and retention. A team incorporates different perspectives, knowledge and personal attributes to inform decision-making, widen understanding and enrich shared learning. An effective team is therefore one that has shared objectives, clear roles and responsibilities, and high levels of participation and communication. Being a member of this sort of team can be characterized as supportive, rewarding, engaging and challenging.

Teams are both a means to provide effective care and means of structuring staff and the work they undertake. The chaplains of an organization constitute a unidisciplinary team within which work can be allocated, tasks assigned, cases discussed or handed on, learning undertaken, information shared and problems discussed. A chaplaincy team may also extend to include locum and honorary members of staff, administration support staff and volunteers. However, chaplains in clinical practice generally work on their own, in close proximity to ward-based teams or as part of multi-disciplinary care teams. For chaplains and other small professional groups, this inevitably introduces the problem of long division: in other words, there is a limit to the number of teams a chaplain can belong to. It is important therefore that chaplains discuss carefully the expectations and responsibilities required of them as members of a team and understand the consequences of this on their wider role and the chaplaincy team as a whole.

Chaplains will have to negotiate daily with many teams in order to respond to their referrals, attend to patients and their carers, understand their needs and provide care. This is often facilitated by establishing good working relationships between a chaplain and individuals in positions of responsibility. It is also supported by chaplaincy departments developing some form of agreed protocols throughout the organization (particularly with nursing and medical colleagues) about access, referrals and the responsibilities of chaplains in relationship to work undertaken within other teams. Healthcare organizations are complex structures of authority, with teams, wards and units exercising considerable power. The lines of responsibility are typically locality based (parochial), which means that there is the potential for them to be more idiosyncratic. Established policy and protocols enable chaplains to operate without contention and with a clear understanding and support of all those with whom they have to work.

Spiritual, religious and pastoral care

Spiritual care is the official term that the NHS uses when it refers to aspects of healthcare that involve religious, pastoral or spiritual dimensions. The term is a category of convenience whose breadth is intended to avoid association with any particular faith community or practice, and therefore be acceptable to the widest number of people. It is also a term derived from the lowest common denominator reasoning that human beings are spiritual and therefore anyone may have spiritual needs. Religious pluralism is an evident characteristic of British society, along with the heterodox beliefs of those who no longer, or never have, observed a religious practice. As a public institution, the NHS must serve the needs of all those who pass through its doors and therefore the language of spiritual care is a practical solution to a dimension of life that many people can relate to in some way or other without being specific.

Spiritual care is not a tidy concept and it has been appropriated by a growing number of health and social care professions. Whatever its theoretical weaknesses, it does provide a way of describing aspects of personhood that are easily dislocated or threatened as a result of disease or trauma: it provides an intelligible discourse for the significant questions of life and death in a health culture pervaded by abstract science and organizational processes, and it offers the space for existential and ethical conversations in a system that can be easily distracted by the apparatus of medicine.

Religious care, in contrast to spiritual care, is more easily described and defined. In this sense it forms a distinct subset of spiritual care and has a clear focus: the practices, doctrines, narratives, experiences, ethics, social organization and material aspects of a faith tradition. Religion is manifest in all societies and its ubiquity demonstrates its usefulness to humanity. In particular, religion is a response to the awareness of a transcendent reality expressed in a framework of meanings by which people can live in relationship to the sacred or the holy. However, in the UK the overall level of religious affiliation has been gradually falling as successive generations have been less actively involved in social aspects of religion – older generations are more religious than younger ones. But while many people are disengaged from religious institutions, forms of belief persist. This ambiguous and at times contradictory situation has been described by Grace Davie as 'believing without belonging', but others question whether these beliefs have any conventionally religious content or even personal significance.

The nature of religion in the UK should ensure caution for any simplistic interpretation of an affiliation declared by a patient to a particular religion or denomination. What are patients expressing about the nature of their beliefs and the relationship they have to a faith community in responding to a blunt question about religion posed to them upon admission to

a healthcare institution? If many people are content to be inactive in religious terms, what happens when they are challenged by ill health? It is evident that in the relatively more
assured arena of religion, a sensitive understanding of the
religious orientation of a person is required that allows for the
varieties of beliefs and practices evident in contemporary
society. However, the pragmatic assumptions that healthcare
staff operate with and the serious limitations of initial assessment processes are often unable to provide the more nuanced
accounts through which the significance, meaning and usefulness of religion for persons and their carers may be understood.

Spiritual care can be contrasted with religious care, but
there is also continuity between them both in practice and in
the conviction that life is meaningful and ultimately sacred
in its nature. It is in response to these larger realities and
deeper possibilities of humanity that chaplains care for people
through a relationship that is primarily pastoral in its nature.
This ministry of care has an essential simplicity in that it seeks
to be helpful and supportive to people in need. In practice,
the nature and scope of pastoral care is expansive and ranges
from psychotherapeutic modes to the performance of religious
ritual. It is also exercised at various social levels from the individual, the relational and the communal. Pastoral care may
therefore be considered as the care of all God's people, and for
chaplains this concern is symbolically expressed in their
responsibility for the spiritual needs of all those in hospital
(patients, carers, staff, students, volunteers and visitors) as
well as for the organization as a whole.

Caring for souls has deep roots in religious traditions, but as
a response to human experience it is unavoidably an evolving
and developing practice. This locates pastoral care in a
place of inevitable but potentially creative tension in that it
addresses the needs of individuals or groups through a discipline grounded in a community of faith. Pastoral care occupies
an ambiguous space: the space between the uniqueness of a
particular situation and the wider historical shared experi-

ences of the communities in which this situation is located and related to. Engaging in these lived experiences and allowing them to speak to and reflect upon one another is at the heart of the pastoral care offered by the chaplain. This dialogue may be unspoken or voiced, but it can only be facilitated by those who are capable of hearing, interpreting and responding to the stories of individuals, the health and social care communities, the faith communities and society. Inevitably this requires the discernment and skill to know where best to be located, how to understand these stories, the nature of language and its limitations, and what it means to be supportive in a particular situation.

Chaplains are not neutral facilitators in the pastoral relationship for they represent socially and symbolically a particular spiritual orientation or worldview. This is what establishes pastoral care as different from other helpful relationships such as informal counselling or psychological support, whose techniques it may draw upon. Pastoral care is the practical embodiment of belief in humanity within a theological framework that is critically sensitive to context and disciplined in its response. As a creative art, pastoral care goes beyond applied technique and has the potential for being nourishing, inspiring and transformational. It also has a wealth of resources at its disposal including the wisdom of faith traditions and their contemplation of the human condition; a challenging theological methodology that strives for truthfulness and authenticity; and religious narratives, myths, symbols, images and rituals that can open up a larger world in which people can discover meaning and hope.

Assessing spiritual care needs

In order to discover a patient's specific needs a range of assessments and diagnostic tests is carried out to determine the treatment or interventions required to help them. A need in medicine is broadly defined by a loss of function and the presence of disease or injury; in a more general sense, a need results from a lack of something or a want. A disease or injury impacts upon the whole of a person's life and it is the person as a whole that hospitals aim to care for. For this reason, the NHS considers that meeting spiritual needs is a fundamental aspect of care, but unless it can be assumed that all patients have needs, and that there are adequate resources for all patients to be seen, then some form of assessment will need to identify who requires spiritual care and in what form.

Clinical pathology and imaging are the bedrock of the diagnostic process which measure, quantify and categorize medical conditions for treatment. This is a highly effective approach to damaged or dysfunctional human biology, but it is insensitive to other aspects of personhood such as human biography and the need for meaning. The simplest approach that hospitals use to understanding something of the spiritual needs of patients is to enquire about a person's religion upon admission. However, given that just over three-quarters of the UK population reported that they had a religion at the last Census (2001), this is a highly rudimentary religious indicator from which only assumptions can be derived that may be inconsistent with the original meaning that the individual intended. It is evident that a more detailed spiritual assessment is required.

Enquiring into the spiritual aspect of a person's life raises a number of ethical issues that need to be considered. It is essential that a spiritual assessment is undertaken with the consent of the patient, either as part of a comprehensive assessment process or as a discrete exercise, and that the purpose and outcome of the assessment are understood by all parties. Spiritual assessments deal with personal information that may contain sensitive material. Issues of confidentiality and disclosure should be understood and a recognized protocol should be followed (see Chapter 8). Engaging a person in a discussion about spirituality may open up highly significant and meaningful aspects of that individual's life that may stimulate heightened feelings and strong reactions. It is important that the person leading the assessment has the knowledge and skills to explore these areas in ways that are respectful,

informed, facilitative and supportive. A patient who indicates
that spirituality has no significance or who expresses discom-
fort when asked should not be subject to further assessment,
but informed of spiritual care support available and the
opportunity to discuss spiritual needs at another time. Finally,
assessing a patient's needs is an ongoing process in healthcare,
and spiritual care needs may change over time and also need
reassessing.

In considering the assessment of spiritual care needs, the
following questions should be considered:

- When should an assessment be initiated and at what level?
- Who should carry out an assessment?
- Is the assessment method practical for the patient/user
  group and the service?
- Is the format and content sensitive to the diversity of
  patients/users?
- Is the assessment method reliable?
- Is the assessment process ethical?
- What follows as a result of the assessment?

Some patients will be confident to present themselves to staff
in terms of their spiritual care needs; other patients will be
reticent to disclose their needs because of their personal
nature, or because they are uncertain of whether the care team
will be responsive to spirituality, or for fear of appearing to be
an unusual or problematic patient. Care teams need to be
proactive in promoting spiritual well-being as an aspect of
care and in ensuring that patients have helpful information
about the chaplaincy service.

Spiritual care assessments rely on the sensitivity and discernment of staff as well as the trust established between the
patient and the health or social care professional. However,
this should be underpinned by a systematic approach to the
assessment of spiritual care that ensures that all patients know
that spiritual well-being is part of healthcare and provides
them with an opportunity to express any spiritual care needs.
Health and social care professionals should be able to

understand, recognize and respond to basic spiritual health needs through the supportive relationships they establish with patients and in the humanity of their care. Staff should also know the limits of their competence in spiritual care and what has the potential to cause distress or harm. They should understand the role of chaplains and know how to make referrals to them. This requires an ongoing educational programme for staff and the provision of effective information. It can also be supported by chaplains developing with their health and social care colleagues relevant indicators that suggest when a referral may be helpful or necessary.

Spirituality, of any depth, does not conform easily to highly systematic forms of assessment, but this does not mean that it should be left to chance or an arbitrary approach. Patients and carers expect to talk to chaplains about spiritual matters and chaplains should be prepared to approach the subject purposefully, sensitively and with understanding. Chaplains need to be committed to dialogue, attentive to listening, open to discerning what cannot be spoken, humble in the presence of another fragile person, and ready to serve through a meaningful encounter. It is through this approach that chaplains can be helpful and supportive to patients, and within the dialogue, silence, gestures and emotions discern something of their spiritual life. Some patients may be direct, but many will approach the subject of spirituality tangentially, with implicit meaning and through symbolic language and imagery. Whatever vocabulary or language is used, the chaplain must engage with the varied expressions of spirituality that a patient uses to enable the person's story to unfold and to care.

One approach that chaplains can find useful is to use a framework of prompts or questions within which to explore spirituality (see Table 4). The framework provides a focus to establish some key aspects of a person's spiritual needs, including:

1 An understanding of the person's spiritual orientation in relation to their life-context.

2 Identifying any practical consequences this may involve in terms of the provision of care.

3 Establishing beliefs or practices that facilitate coping and factors that may hinder spiritual well-being.

4 Recognizing the significance of beliefs in the experience of injury or illness and in making healthcare decisions.

5 Determining any support or resources needed.

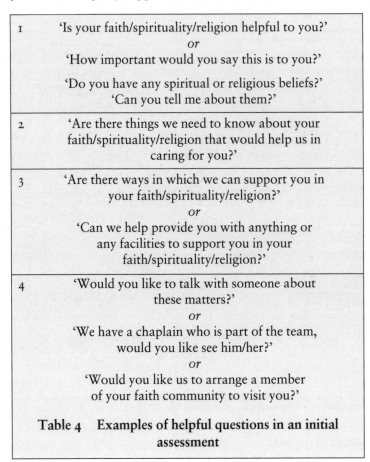

1	'Is your faith/spirituality/religion helpful to you?' *or* 'How important would you say this is to you?' 'Do you have any spiritual or religious beliefs?' 'Can you tell me about them?'
2	'Are there things we need to know about your faith/spirituality/religion that would help us in caring for you?'
3	'Are there ways in which we can support you in your faith/spirituality/religion?' *or* 'Can we help provide you with anything or any facilities to support you in your faith/spirituality/religion?'
4	'Would you like to talk with someone about these matters?' *or* 'We have a chaplain who is part of the team, would you like see him/her?' *or* 'Would you like us to arrange a member of your faith community to visit you?'

Table 4   Examples of helpful questions in an initial assessment

Two practical paper-based exercises may also be helpful in exploring the wider context in which the person lives. The first of these is a genogram, or family-tree, which can help a patient

Genogram symbols

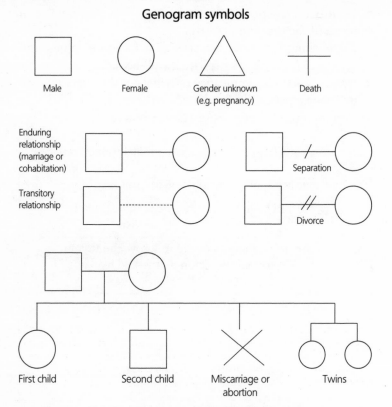

A dotted line should be drawn around the people who currently live in the same house.

Figure 5   The symbols of a genogram and how they are connected

explain who they are related to both in terms of those in the immediate proximity as well as those distanced by space and time (see Figure 5). The genogram at its simplest is a representation of the patient's relatives, but it can also be the means for a patient to tell the stories of what these relationships mean. The second exercise is an ecomap, which is a visual representation of social information about a patient (see Figure 6). Unlike the genogram, the ecomap can include friends, neigh-

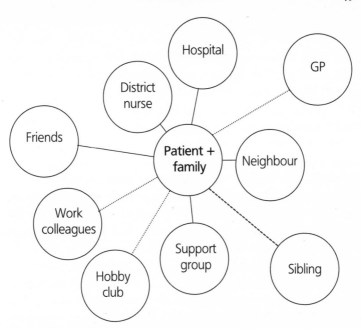

The patient and their family system is placed at the centre of the diagram. More circles are added to represent socially significant people or systems. Lines are then drawn to represent the relationships between the elements. Dotted lines represent more tenuous relationships. Zig-zag lines represent contentious or difficult relationships. Arrows may be added to represent the direction of support.

Figure 6   An example of an ecomap

bours, work colleagues, pets and other significant people such as the GP, social worker or minister. The ecomap provides a diagram of the person in the context of their wider social environment and can also include significant organizations such as the hospital. Different lines can be used between the elements of the ecomap to indicate supportive or difficult links. Drawing either of these diagrams is an activity in which both the chaplain and the patient can participate, and it can also involve any significant visitors whom the patient may want to include. Both exercises can help illustrate the resources that support the patient as well as the people or systems that are problematic.

Caring for the person in context

The main focus of much healthcare and of chaplaincy is the individual in need. When a person is suffering the immediate effects of a trauma or acute illness, attention is rightly given to the patient, or sometimes particular parts of the patient, in order to arrest or reverse the damaging consequences of their condition. This individualistic and internalized approach to care is restrictive and neglects the wider relational, social and cultural horizons that health and well-being are related to and dependent upon. An ecological approach understands the individual within a context of close relationships (e.g. family, carers and friends), local contacts and the environment (e.g. work colleagues and the neighbourhood), and the wider social, economic, educational, political and legal systems (the nation). The person in context is an expansive picture of interplay and interdependence between a complex set of variables which, understood as a system, sees the problems experienced by individuals as interconnected with and therefore influenced by other parts of the whole.

To provide effective care to the individual requires understanding something of the person in the context of their world. Conversely, understanding the broader picture suggests where problems may arise and what may be factors in their cause. For example, if we consider the population of the UK then we see an ageing population (resulting from a decrease in the birth rate and an increase in life expectancy), which in turn increases the risk of cancer. About one-third of the population will be diagnosed with cancer at some stage in their life; half of these cases will be breast, lung, colorectal or prostate cancer; two-thirds of cases will occur in those aged over 65; and about a quarter of all people diagnosed with cancer will die from the disease. This has implications for the number of people chaplains are likely to encounter who have cancer, the symptoms they have, and the life-issues they are dealing with. There are also social factors that can be considered as part of this picture and which also impact upon spiritual care: around

3 in 10 households consist of one person and another 3 in 10 consist of couples with no children. This may have implications about the limited extent of the family network that may be able to offer support to someone who is unwell.

Social studies, demographics, epidemiology and other analyses of the wider contexts in which people live provide chaplains with an informed understanding of the factors that impact upon people and that contribute to pastoral and spiritual needs. This in turn may inform the response of chaplains to those they care for. For example, consider Margaret who has been admitted to an acute medical ward after being brought to Accident and Emergency following a collapse in the residential home she lives in. On Sunday, Margaret requests to be taken to the hospital chapel where she meets the chaplain taking the service. In conversation, the chaplain discovers that Margaret is an Anglican and receives a monthly visit from a Reader in the local parish. It appears that Margaret simply wants to maintain the observance of her religious practice. But when we consider Margaret within the broader picture of her world, we see an older woman, with a history of epilepsy and periods of major depression, who has spent much of her life in institutional care and most of her earlier life in a large psychiatric hospital. Her only relative is a niece who visits her about twice a year. Margaret's epilepsy and depression have created genuine difficulties for her, but many of the problems she has faced have been a result of the values and assumptions of society and the beliefs and structures of services. Consequently Margaret has been viewed as deeply problematic and been subject to prejudice, discrimination, social disadvantage and exclusion. These messages have been internalized by Margaret and incorporated into her beliefs.

The chaplain's first encounter with Margaret is in the chapel in which both participate in a religious service that expresses something of the story of the faith community in hymns, readings, prayers, ritual and sacrament. In subsequent encounters with Margaret, the chaplain brings this story into dialogue with Margaret's own story, not directly, but by opening up a space between them where the connections, contradictions and possibilities can be explored. Margaret's religious observance has been very important to her throughout her life; indeed, it has been one of the few continuities that she has had, and the chaplain must therefore treat this commitment with great sensitivity and respect. But the chaplain can also hold open space for the doubt, the hurts, the confusion and the vital questions that arise for people about themselves and their faith as a result of suffering or trauma. For Margaret, this safe and supportive space enabled her to discover new insights into her own story and that of the faith community which motivated her to consider afresh how she wanted to live her life and what she expected from those who cared for her. In particular, she rediscovered her true sense of value and dignity and she began to understand that her epilepsy was part of who she was and not a problematic affliction that she should be ashamed of. She went on to meet with a psychiatrist who went through her early notes with her and explained the treatment she had received. And she asked her home to arrange for her to attend services in her local church and to be included in outings and other social functions.

The transforming and empowering potential of spiritual care goes beyond meeting initial needs when it is cognizant and critically aware of the contexts in which people live their lives. If chaplains aim to promote the spiritual well-being of patients, then they will need to attend to the wider factors that diminish persons and disrespect their human value. This wider institutional and social role may be an uncomfortable place for chaplains to be in, but it is a place of integrity related to their encounters with individuals and with their faith community. It is also a place of theological integrity in which the demands of truth and justice require creative engagement with the situation, an openness to new interpretations, fresh insights and revelation, and a commitment to change what harms and damages people.

4

Care across the Life-course

Chaplains are involved with caring for people at all stages along the course of life – from the cradle to the grave. This provides a contextual framework to help us consider some significant healthcare themes and their related spiritual issues which can be associated with particular stages or places on the life-course or to transitions between stages. In this chapter we consider this contextual method and relate it to four examples of the life-course approach:

- Pregnancy and childbirth.
- Mental health.
- Critical care.
- Older people.

Spiritual care in the context of the life-course

To live is to change and in this sense people are continually negotiating transitions in their lives, but there are key places on the life-course that provide major themes for a particular age group, gender or life-experience in relation to healthcare need: for example, childhood, pregnancy or dementia. These places offer a useful (although artificial) focus with which to understand the basis of spiritual care that locates the individual within a wider context of influences including the social and cultural, biographical or life-history, psychological, and personal beliefs and values. What this suggests is that meaningful and beneficial spiritual care needs to be located in context, and this requires that chaplains have some level of understanding of the factors that may be contributing to a situation and how to modulate spiritual care to achieve its aims in a particular situation.

Locating spiritual care in a context requires a disciplined approach or method that facilitates critical reflection upon the experience of an individual or group. The chaplain thus requires the ability to understand the language, practices, values and beliefs expressed through the stories of individuals and the healthcare community within their wider social contexts. As a process this is best described as theological reflection because it opens the way for a dialogue about meaning and belief in relationship to the normative faith tradition in which the chaplain is fluent. Understanding, analysis, detailed reflection and new insights are then reapplied to the situation and integrated into revised practice. From this, fresh questions may emerge, new practices are developed and the spiritual care dialogue is enriched.

There is no neutral approach to spiritual care because we all start from somewhere, and for chaplains this includes their own faith, beliefs and life-experience; their ethical values and goals; and their understanding and assumptions about subjects such as health, suffering and death. This particular worldview will influence and shape the approach of the chaplain to the people encountered in healthcare and the stories and situations they present. It is through our worldview that we interpret our experiences, make sense of other people, and structure our actions.

People's spiritual well-being is further influenced by their experience of systems of care and the implicit and expressed spiritual values of the healthcare institutions and organizations.

Pregnancy and childbirth

The beginning of life is a subject surrounded by contentious theological and ethical questions that have serious pastoral implications. The questions of when human life begins and what constitutes a human person find a range of answers in biology, law and religion. Perhaps the crucial issue concerns the moral status of the developing embryo, how this is recognized, and the duties this implies. When the chromosomes of a human egg and sperm combine at fertilization, then a genetically unique cell is created that has the potential to develop into a baby. At this stage, some argue that human life is created that should be fully respected as a human person; others argue that the moral status of the individual develops along with certain capacities such as sentience, self-consciousness and rational thought.

Beliefs concerning the moral status of a baby have implications for a range of issues including assisted reproduction, pre-natal screening, neonatal treatment, pregnancy loss, abortion and perinatal deaths (see Table 5). Chaplains may often be involved with parents when there is a conflict between beliefs and when people are uncertain about what decision they should take. Parents may want to talk through issues and receive advice from a particular religious perspective or they may want the opportunity to talk through a decision that has profound consequences with someone that they consider will understand and listen to them. Chaplains may also be called upon, or offer, religious rituals and ceremonies in celebration of life and to honour its ending (see Liturgy in Chapter 9).

The pastoral encounters that chaplains have around pregnancy often require the holding of conflicting emotions, thoughts and expectations, some of which derive from the contradiction of social norms by actual experience. The notion of the family in particular may be an underlying theme whose complexities a chaplain must be capable of dealing with. The decline in marriage and the increase in divorce mean that over 40 per cent of births are to unmarried couples, of whom around three-quarters are cohabiting. In addition, assisted reproduction techniques can mean that there is no link between the child's genetic and legal parents. In pastoral situations, it is important that the 'family' tree is understood as much as it can be, in order to avoid embarrassment and

Embryo – baby from three weeks of pregnancy onwards.

Foetus – baby from eight weeks of pregnancy onwards.

Miscarriage or early pregnancy loss – babies born dead before 24 completed weeks' gestation.

Stillbirth – babies born dead after 24 or more weeks' completed gestation.

Perinatal death – baby who is stillborn or dies within the first seven days of life.

Neonatal death – death in the first four weeks of life.

Tremester – a three-month period, used by healthcare professionals, to describe the first, second and third stages of pregnancy.

Viability – at 24 weeks' gestation, a baby is called 'viable', which means that the lungs and other vital organs are well enough developed to allow a good chance of survival if the baby is born.

Weeks of pregnancy – pregnancy is counted in weeks from the first day of a woman's last menstrual period (not from conception). Pregnancy normally lasts between 37 and 42 weeks, with an average of 40 weeks (usually written 40/52).

Table 5   Terminology used in pregnancy

offence where biological or legal facts are not necessarily coherent with social reality. It is also necessary when discussing choices (for example, whether or not to baptize a baby) to establish parentage and therefore who is entitled to take decisions. In general, the woman who gives birth to a child will be regarded as the legal mother. (The commissioning parents of a surrogate mother must apply to the courts to obtain the legal status of parents of the child whose birth they had arranged.) The man who provides the sperm that leads to the conception of a baby is usually regarded as the father unless the man was a sperm donor, in which case the mother's 'partner' is usually treated as the father.

In providing care for people in pregnancy and childbirth, chaplains should aim to work alongside the other health and social care professionals involved. This can help to ensure a consistent understanding of complex situations, care that is co-ordinated around the needs of parents and their families, and mutual support for staff in dealing with stressful circumstances. An example of this is the tragic situation of distressed parents who arrive at Accident and Emergency one night with a young baby who has stopped breathing. The baby is examined by a doctor and the parents are informed that the baby is dead and it is explained to them that young babies are at a very vulnerable stage in their development, and that the most common cause of deaths in infants aged from one month to one year is known as cot death, or Sudden Infant Death Syndrome (SIDS).

The parents are concerned that their baby has not been baptized and the chaplain on duty is called (see Liturgy in Chapter 9). The police are also called because the law requires that all sudden and unexpected deaths are investigated and it is usual for the police (acting on behalf of the coroner or procurator fiscal) to speak with the parents, to remove items of clothing and bedding for forensic tests, take photographs, and sometimes visit the home. In this situation the chaplain must work closely with all those involved to ensure that the spiritual and pastoral needs of the parents can be met with dignity and respect. The chaplain may also have a role in debriefing the staff and the police in Accident and Emergency and supporting them in an emotionally and spiritually demanding situation.

Mental health

The World Health Organization considers that there is no health without mental health and that mental and physical health are interdependent. Mental health is the basis for well-being, effective functioning and the contribution that individuals can make to their communities. Conversely, communities contribute to the mental health of individuals, and social factors – along with psychological and biological factors – are related to mental illness: for example, there is a strong association between poverty and mental disorders. Mental health problems are common (one in four people) and universal, they are surrounded by stigma, and they have (historically) been treated separately from other forms of healthcare. Chaplains, in whichever sector of healthcare they are working, will therefore have to deal with issues relating to mental health.

The language of mental health and the practices of mental healthcare operate within some commonly held assumptions about the nature and meaning of what constitutes mental illness. This paradigm uses a system of classification that seeks to distinguish between mental health and illness; however, some argue that there are no clear boundaries or diagnoses, but simply psychological complaints and experiences that trouble some people and that exist on continua with normal behaviours and experience. The unusual beliefs and experiences of some people considered to be living with mental health problems (for example, hallucinations, delusional beliefs, incoherent speech and mood swings) have often been interpreted by societies in ways that have stigmatized, excluded and disenfranchised these people. However, increasingly new approaches are being made that both recognize the breadth of human diversity and variance while addressing distressing psychological complaints in ways that are sensitive to more than biological factors. Listening to people with mental health problems, how they value their experiences and respecting their own opinions about the effects of treatments, has undoubtedly contributed to this shift.

Religion has been associated with mental illness as both a cause and a symptom. People's experiences of religion can be damaging and contribute to mental health problems. People with mental illnesses may experience religion in ways that are distorted or a focus for their delusions. But spiritual beliefs and religious activity can also have psychological benefits and there is a growing research literature that suggests positive clinical associations of spiritual beliefs and religious involvement with mental health. The primary concern for the chaplain must be the lived experience of the individual as a person and not a patient with a diagnostic label ('the depressive'). In acute settings, people with mental health problems can often be further labelled 'problem patients' when they contradict the norm of the compliant and grateful recipient of care. In accepting the person as authentic, the chaplain is able to offer the possibility of a space not shaped by stigma in which the individual can relate his or her story without prejudice. Sharing a story is one way to forge a caring relationship and this in itself may be empowering. More in-depth work may involve exploring spiritual beliefs and experiences and considering the resources that spirituality and religion may have to offer.

The focus of the chaplain in the pastoral encounter will be the individual person, but the wider social and cultural factors that contribute to mental health suggest that spiritual care related to mental health must also attend to these more systemic and cultural issues. This may result, for example, in educational work by the chaplain within the healthcare organization aimed at reducing stigma and discrimination, or developing a befriending service to patients who are socially isolated, or contributing to stress reduction programmes. The chaplain may also be in a good position to build networks between the healthcare organization and local faith and voluntary communities that can contribute to reducing the social isolation of people with mental health problems and offer practical help and supportive care.

Critical care

Patients with acute, life-threatening illnesses or injuries are provided with critical care which is usually delivered in specialized units and centres (for example, high dependency and intensive care units) by multidisciplinary teams. In addition to life-threatening illnesses, critical care includes serious trauma (resulting from accidents, injuries and wounds), surgical complications, poisoning, severe myocardial infarctions and strokes. The aim of critical care is to halt or reverse acute physiological deterioration, and therefore some patients may benefit more from intensive care on the ward or palliative care.

The nature of critical care means that patients are at a high risk of death and require advanced support and high levels of care to address acute problems such as respiratory and circulatory failure or progressive organ dysfunction. Patients are usually subject to proactive management, detailed observation and often rapid treatment and interventions. This can be a highly distressing environment for visitors in which the patient may be sedated, intubated and connected to various monitors and infusion pumps. Access to the patient can be difficult, communication is hindered because of the noise of equipment, and visiting is often limited because of the need for staff to carry out procedures and perform care.

A common role for chaplains in critical care is to support visitors having to face the life-threatening condition of someone they care about. This may involve dealing with people who are fearful, anxious, distressed, guilty, angry, and in a state of shock. This requires well-developed communication skills and often high levels of interaction in order to understand people and to provide support. Critical situations also benefit from focused attention to all the senses to gain a more comprehensive insight into an individual's state when verbal communication is difficult or inhibited by emotions. Chaplains also need to be aware of the feelings that critical care generates in them as well as the feelings that their role may generate in others. In particular, people may see the chaplain in terms of how they think of God. A person may have a negative view of God as one who has abandoned or punished them, or the individual may view God positively as one who can intervene and rescue people from difficult situations. Whatever the view of God, it will find some transference on to the chaplain who must deal with the mistaken identity and also work with the person's understanding and experience of God.

Patients who are critically ill or injured are at risk of dying and a major pastoral theme in critical care is mortality or the frail and fragile nature of human existence. Most people depend upon a considerable level of certainty and stability in life and in other people, and a critical event can challenge this. Such a loss of prediction and control can destabilize a person's worldview and question their own security. It can also be an opportunity for people to reflect more deeply upon the impermanent nature of human existence and the ultimate meaning and purpose of life. The chaplain can provide a safe space in which to explore issues of mortality and reflect upon the beliefs of a faith tradition. Questions concerning mortality may also be addressed in the discussions that relatives and friends are involved in regarding end-of-life decisions. In England and Wales, only doctors can take decisions for adult patients who are no longer competent to decide for themselves. But the views of carers are often sought, and the new Mental Capacity Act (2005) provides for people to appoint an attorney of their choosing to act on their behalf, including taking decisions of health and personal welfare, if they should lose capacity in the future. In Scotland, a proxy decision-maker may be appointed who can give consent to, or refuse, medical treatment on behalf of the adult. Chaplains may be called upon to facilitate these discussions and offer ethical advice.

Older people

Lower birth rates and lower mortality rates are shifting the balance of generations: there are more people aged over 60 than there are children under 16. Approximately one in five people in the UK is aged 65 or over (11 million people) and people over 85 constitute the fastest growing segment of the population. It should be noted that, in general, people from ethnic minority groups have a much younger age structure.

Many diseases and disabilities are related to the ageing process that makes people's bodies more vulnerable to pathology and dysfunction. As people live longer, there is also an epidemiological transition from acute infections to chronic conditions such as diabetes, cancer and cardiovascular disease. These often have an impact upon people's mobility and independence, which in turn makes those individuals more reliant upon carers – who are often family and friends. More than two-thirds of people over 60 report some measure of disability, and over half of the estimated 5.7 million carers in Britain are looking after people aged 75 or over. Consequently, older people are the majority of users (two-thirds) of acute care services and they also have particular mental health and social care needs.

Ageing has many ambivalent and negative stereotypes associated with it, representing inexorable decline and negativity in contrast to the positive and vital images of youth. Older people are easily ostracized because they do not fit into the dominant social scripts; equally, few of us foresee our ageing and most of us hold it as an abstract rather than an inevitably embodied fact. Older people are easily counted as of decreasing value to society except in terms of the cost of health and social care, and the older person can feel a burden with a sense of diminishing self-worth. Society does not as a whole cherish older people and affirm their dignity and worth as persons. For example, older people are not considered (superficially) beautiful, but we may see and appreciate a deeper beauty in the maturity of their character, experience and wisdom.

In seeking to meet the spiritual needs of older people it is helpful to understand the person in the context of both their immediate social network, their wider social experiences and their history. Old age is a continuation of a person's biographical life, not a disjoined episode, and an older person's significant past may continue to be reflected in the individual's present and give shape to the future. However, to varying degrees, the lives of older people are challenged by change over which they may have little control but that may diminish or threaten the person's sense of identity, purpose, significance, belonging and relatedness to others. These temporal and relational perspectives provide a useful focus in understanding the spiritual care needs of older people and can often provide helpful prompts in seeking to learn from the expertise of both the older person and his or her carers.

A discontinuity that older people can often face is a disconnection from their faith community that may have resulted from their immobility, their relocation resulting from a move to a care home, or as a result of progressive cognitive impairment such as memory loss or confusion. It should be relatively easy for a hospital chaplain to find ways to support the older person in his or her religious beliefs and practices, but it may be considerably more difficult to negotiate with a local faith community to find ways for the person to continue participating. Cognitive impairment can present particular challenges in spiritual care, requiring a chaplain to develop additional knowledge, understanding and skills. An example of this is caring for people with dementia whose symptoms may include memory loss, mood changes and communication problems. People experience dementia in different ways, but they remain unique individuals. In providing spiritual care for people with dementia, chaplains should seek to promote their value and sense of self through giving them time and finding ways to connect with them in the present moment; in showing understanding when they are anxious or distressed; by explaining who you are, what you are doing and offering choice; and by communicating at an appropriate pace that is aware of body language and is sensitive to the meaning of what is being expressed and its feeling.

Spiritual care can contribute to the quality of life of older people at individual, social and societal levels. On a ward, in a unit or in a care home chaplains can contribute to and foster an environment of spiritual care in their contact with individual patients, carers and staff that enables a greater sensitivity to the spiritual dimension and supports meaningful responses. Chaplains can develop relationships and social activities that express the value of spirituality in the identity of older people and recognize that people can continue to grow spiritually. The life-affirming character of spiritual care can have positive consequences for people's mental health, the quality and meaning of caring relationships, and the creative resourcefulness of services provided for people who because of their age may be vulnerable, fragile and often disregarded by society.

5

The Care and Support of Bereaved People

A significant aspect of the ministry of a chaplain will be among those facing the death of someone significant to them, or who have already been bereaved. This chapter provides a basic introduction to the nature of grief and the care of the bereaved:

- Understanding death and bereavement.
- Expressions of grief.
- Complicated grief.
- Listening to the stories of grief.
- Follow-up care.
- Support and care beyond the health service.

Understanding death and bereavement

Most people die in healthcare settings and many of these deaths will occur in acute hospitals as a result of diseases of the circulatory and respiratory systems, as well as neoplasms. Bearing witness to the consequence of fatal pathological events and supporting carers is therefore an inevitable part of the clinical practice of chaplains. In the presence of death we face the significance of human absence and loss, the deprivation of future possibilities, and the emptiness of an embodied space once filled with life. More immediately, chaplains are often requested to administer sacraments, pray commendations and offer spiritual care and pastoral support to the bereaved. Most acute hospitals do not have well-resourced bereavement support services beyond the practicalities necessary for the disposal of deceased patients. In addition, professional boundaries, the discontinuities between care settings and the relatively brief encounters carers have with acute health services often lead to the limited availability of bereavement care. It is in this context that chaplains may be called to care for people facing loss or those who have already been bereaved.

One way of understanding bereavement is as a life-event that requires us to revise and renegotiate the world we live in. Many of the expectations, assumptions and meanings by which we navigate our lives and orientate ourselves can be disrupted or invalidated as a result of bereavement. It can therefore become necessary to relearn the world, not simply to take account of the absence of the person who has died, but because the death of an individual can have a pervasive impact upon who we are and how we live. This requires attending to more than our psychological dimension and may involve relearning the physical, temporal, spiritual and social aspects of our world. Relearning implies change and this can be a creative, positive and fruitful exercise. However, bereavement can also be a challenging or stressful transition in that it makes demands upon people beyond their resources as they attempt to deal with loss and renegotiate a meaningful life without the deceased.

In offering bereavement care and support, chaplains should be aware of the conceptual models of bereavement and loss that inform and guide their clinical practice. A conventional model understands bereavement as a necessary process to relinquish the object of love, restore equilibrium and psychological stability, to resume life and establish new relationships. According to this model, it is detachment or letting go of the dead person that is the primary task of grief in order that the bereaved person may re-engage and reinvest in life. So-called normal grief would therefore be determined by the successful withdrawal of energy from the lost object according to a predetermined pattern, whereas avoidance, suppression or denial of this task may determine pathological grief. However, it has become increasingly apparent that this type of model has many limitations, not least in its narrow focus on the individual, the emotional effect of grief, the predetermined stages and characteristics of mourning, and the expectation of resolution within a given time.

Chaplains are guided and influenced by theories and by their own experiences, training, beliefs, attitudes and assumptions. As with other aspects of pastoral support, they need to develop and maintain a level of self-awareness and self-knowledge about areas of their own lives that are potential sources of difficulty or conflict in bereavement situations. People who are bereaved may become subject to the needs of the chaplain who is living out, through either conscious or unconscious processes, their own bereavement. Equally, chaplains may develop strategies and practices that avoid or minimize the possibility or impact of caring for the bereaved when painful personal loss is evoked. For this reason it is helpful for bereavement care and support to be the subject of supervision where the impact of the chaplain's personal experience of bereavement can be safely explored in relationship to pastoral practice.

It is important that chaplains are able to maintain a wider perspective on how people cope with bereavement. Loss and change are unavoidable aspects of life, and consequently people have to negotiate many types of disruptions and dislocations to their world over the years. In this sense, bereavement is a normal situation that people find themselves in and that most will cope with and learn to live with. They do this without any particular professional intervention, but they may often receive support and care from those they are in close proximity to. Family, friends and colleagues are often well placed to provide accessible and practical help as well as to respond to the times when companionship and a sympathetic ear are required.

Expressions of grief

All people have a finite future, and death is an event that applies to all of us. However, the grief reaction of people can appear to be markedly different to this ubiquitous experience in terms of the way it is expressed, the intensity of suffering and the period for which it lasts. For these reasons, becoming involved with bereaved people requires chaplains to develop a broad understanding of the impact of loss upon personhood that is sensitive not only to psychological insights, but also to other significant aspects of their social context, beliefs, history, gender, ethnicity and culture. The expressions of grief can include cognitive, emotional, somatic and social manifestations (see Table 6) which are common for most – but not all – people in the early months following the loss.

The death of someone significant can have a disorganizing impact upon a bereaved person that is manifest in difficulties with understanding and making sense of loss. This search for meaning and for answers to the question 'Why?' are often long term. Those who are bereaved also talk of finding it hard to believe that the death has happened, and some report being preoccupied with memories and images of the deceased person. An associated phenomenon is the impact of the loss upon the identity of the bereaved person, in which they feel part of them has died. Related to these cognitive experiences is the prevalence of dysphoric and distressing emotions, typically those of sadness and anger among a range of emotional states. In addition, bereaved people commonly yearn or pine for the person who has died and experience a strong sense of loneliness.

Bereavement is often a very stressful experience that can have negative health consequences. The bereaved often report significantly greater health complaints and worsened, or new, illnesses. These may be exacerbated by increased drinking or smoking following bereavement, and there may be a higher risk of alcohol and substance misuse. There are also some bereaved people who are at risk of developing enduring

Feelings
- Sadness
- Anger
- Guilt and self-reproach
- Anxiety
- Loneliness
- Fatigue

- Helplessness
- Shock
- Yearning
- Emancipation
- Relief
- Numbness

Physical sensations

Cognitions
- Disbelief
- Confusion
- Preoccupation

- Sense of presence
- Hallucinations

Behaviours
- Sleep disturbances
- Appetite disturbances
- Absent-minded behaviour
- Social withdrawal
- Dreams of the deceased
- Avoiding reminders of the deceased
- Searching and calling out

- Sighing
- Restless over-activity
- Crying
- Visiting places or carrying objects that remind the survivor of the deceased
- Treasuring objects that belonged to the deceased

Source: J. W. Worden, *Grief Counselling and Grief Therapy*
(Brunner-Routledge, 2003).

Table 6   Some manifestations of grief

mental health problems. In addition to bereavement-related depression and anxiety, some people may develop symptoms related to separation and traumatic distress. In a small number of cases, the severity of despair and hopelessness may lead to suicidal ideas and thoughts.

People who are bereaved can have difficulties in fulfilling their usual social and occupational roles and may become withdrawn and emotionally unavailable for a period. Bereavement can impact upon the roles people have in their family and in their careers, as well as bringing about changes in daily life activities and routines which can be difficult to manage for some people. An individual's expression of grief can also have a negative impact upon those who may be expected to provide social support, but who may choose to avoid the pain and distress of the bereaved person. There is also evidence that conjugally bereaved individuals have temporary difficulties developing new intimate relationships. Women appear to take longer to engage in these sorts of relationships, and men are more likely to remarry.

A significant personal loss is usually associated with negative experiences, but there are also positive aspects of bereavement. Facing someone's death and mourning the loss may be evaluated by some people as more of a positive experience through which they have learnt and grown as an individual. The loss of the relationship can be a release for some people, and others begin to appreciate the new freedom. In addition to positive thoughts, there may also be positive emotional experiences. The death of a significant person may come as a relief and people may find consolation in their religious or spiritual beliefs about the deceased person's destiny. Bereaved people may also experience a pride in the person who has died and be comforted by the love and affection they still have for them. People who are bereaved may also find great pleasure in their memories and enjoy recounting stories.

Complicated grief

Bereavement results in diverse reactions in people, with considerable variation in the manifestations of grief. Within this spectrum, it is recognized that for some people bereavement may affect their health and well-being to such an extent that there may be a justification for psychological or pharmacological interventions. Prolonged or extreme reactions to bereavement may be considered abnormal or complicated in comparison to a standard model, and diagnostic criteria have been proposed for bereavement-related pathologies and disorders. However, there is also caution because many negative symptoms of bereavement are expected and typical, people who are bereaved can experience high levels of suffering and still cope, and there is a danger in oversimplifying the effects of bereavement and deciding that it must be problematic.

Most people exhibit patterns of *common grief* that cause moderate disruption to their lives in the early months following a bereavement. Some people manifest few or no signs of loss, and this *minimal grief* may be a normal response for them. But it has also been estimated that for approximately 15 per cent of bereaved people, disruptive experiences of grief persist rather than gradually decline. Enduring serious disruption as a result of bereavement can be considered a form of *chronic grief*, which becomes evident in unresolved or complicated symptoms. If these people can be identified, then it is possible to give them the support and attention they need – and for this reason there are attempts to establish diagnostic criteria to enable targeted preventative work and interventions. It may also be possible to identify people who are at a higher risk of developing complicated grief reactions before a death has occurred. A common approach to predicting someone's vulnerability to bereavement is the use of a risk assessment, which aims to consider the cumulative impact of certain factors for the individual (see Table 7).

A chaplain may come to know and understand much about the person who is bereaved and the circumstances of the death, and can therefore be a key member of staff in exploring possible vulnerability and suggesting means of support. However, it may be much later after the death that a bereaved person feels that they are in difficulty or that they present to a health service with symptoms of complicated grief. A common source of help for these people is counselling, which is widely available through GP practices, voluntary agencies and private practices. The evidence suggests that counselling in primary care is useful in the short-term treatment of mild to moderate mental health problems, and has some positive effect when used for complicated grief. But grief counselling and therapy may only be of help to a small number of bereaved people, and

---

Situational
- How did the individual experience and react to the illness and death?
- Are there any concurrent life-events that may cause additional stress?

Individual
- Who has been lost?
- What is the meaning of the lost relationship?
- How is the individual's life-experience and personality affecting their reactions and way of coping?
- Are there any pre-existing psychological or physical health problems?

Environmental
- How much support is available and to what extent is it perceived as helpful?

Source: M. Relf, 'Risk Assessment and Bereavement Service', in Payne, S., Seymour, J. and Ingleton, C. (eds), *Palliative Care Nursing* (Open University Press, 2004).

Table 7   Key risk factors when assessing a person's capacity to cope with a bereavement

---

in particular those who have requested this type of help and who may be vulnerable to complicated grief.

Listening to the stories of grief

The loss of a significant person can disrupt – and, for some, devastate – the world of meaning, which provides necessary purpose and direction to life. A world changed by death challenges existing meanings and beliefs while presenting demanding questions of why the death occurred and what its significance might be both for the person who has died and the bereaved. One way that people who are bereaved search for significance and meaning in death is through the narration of their experience. One model suggests three particular types of narrative that people use. First, there are objective forms that provide descriptions and reports of what has happened. The objective form of these narratives provides ordered versions of external events from a personal perspective and therefore also relate to the storyteller. Descriptions of how the person died, reporting the actions of individuals and recounting what happened at the funeral are examples of external narratives. Second, there are internal narratives that focus upon the affective responses to the death as experienced by the narrator or biographer. These self-expressions of what it feels like to experience the loss are emotion-based narratives and articulate the internal world of the bereaved person. Third, there are reflexive narratives that build upon the primary narratives – recalling what happened or expressing feeling – and provide a secondary narrative of interpretation and reflection. Exploring the significance of the death, why it happened and what the death means to the storyteller are examples of reflexive narratives.

Listening to the life-stories of people and helping them to narrate their experiences is a core chaplaincy skill, and it can be a helpful approach to supporting bereaved people. Most people can tell stories, but some people will choose to remain solitary in their grief; a narrative may not be formed in spoken or written words, and silence may be just as important to someone as dialogue. If death imposes an absence, then for some people bereavement may not require anything to be said about it other than what is evident. Storytelling must not be an imperative to fill the silence. Equally we must resist the social convention of making people talk, and we should question a professional convention that automatically refers the inarticulate to counsellors and therapists. Mourning tends to make people more self-absorbed, as well as in need of other people, and this private experience may not find an account that can be communicated.

Narratives of loss are ongoing projects and people who are bereaved may revise and revisit them individually and in association with others. Chaplains may also share in the stories of bereaved people because they may be part of the story. A person may need to establish a coherent account of how someone became ill and died with those who hold records and memories of such events. A bereaved person may also feel confident in describing their feelings to someone who they expect might understand how people respond to loss. In this way, a bereaved person may be checking out their own position and seeking validation for their feelings, thoughts and beliefs. Chaplains may also be turned to by bereaved people because they are assumed to understand the context of loss and therefore may be able to assist in conserving what has gone, while negotiating what it means to live in the changed world. This context is both temporal and spiritual, and people may be seeking help in narrating their experience and searching for meaning within a framework of beliefs about human destiny and ultimate purpose.

Follow-up care

Most people do not die suddenly, and from diagnosis to death both patients and carers may receive the support of professionals. Even death resulting from acute events and undiagnosed conditions can often be accompanied by chaplains and other health professionals. However, many health services come to a halt following a death, with the exception of some specialist services, of which palliative care is a particular example. Professional and service boundaries can impose their own disruption and discontinuity upon bereaved people. People who are bereaved can therefore find themselves estranged from both the context in which death has taken place and those professionals who they may expect to understand what it is that they are experiencing.

In the immediate period following a death there are many tasks that require the involvement of the bereaved, principally the funeral, which brings them to the attention of others, including chaplains and ministers of religion. This can establish a transient cluster of support and people to turn to for help and advice. But within weeks this level of support has usually withdrawn and bereaved people may experience a further ending of care. What may help bereaved people through these significant transitions are relatively simple follow-up contacts that chaplains may be involved with. These can take the form of telephone calls, letters and cards, as well as domiciliary visits where there are adequate resources. The purpose of these contacts can include: the expression of concern regarding the well-being of the bereaved; an opportunity for the bereaved to say something of their current feelings and experiences; the opportunity for them to raise questions or concerns either about the death or the bereavement; the provision of information about sources of bereavement support in the community; the offer of further follow-up; and a means of ending the involvement of a service.

Follow-up contacts should form part of a systematic approach to bereavement by a health service so that they are co-ordinated and adequately supported by staff competent in dealing with bereaved people. A bereavement aftercare programme introduced into one emergency department aimed to be easily absorbed into existing workloads, beneficial and unobtrusive as possible to the bereaved, and offering some continuity with staff present at the time of the person's death. The follow-up aspect of this programme involved sending a handwritten sympathy card to the closest relative and a follow-up phone call at one week (to assess needs) and at six weeks (which relatives could decline). The hospital received much positive feedback from those enrolled on the programme who had appreciated that staff cared about them. It was also considered to be a beneficial process for the staff involved as it allowed them to demonstrate a more human side of healthcare.

Another form of follow-up that chaplains are often involved in organizing and leading are memorial events and associated services. These are usually connected with specialist services and focus upon people who are bereaved through a similar type of death – for example, bereaved parents. While the majority of memorial events are planned to provide a regular opportunity for bereaved people to gather and remember the dead, some events are more spontaneous and are held subsequent to the death of a member of staff or student or following a major tragedy. Planning such an event can be a major task; there are often many practical issues to be addressed and a variety of resources that need mobilizing. It is also important to anticipate the level of support that people attending the service may require and to have suitably trained or qualified staff available. The creative rituals that often feature in memorial events can be helpful and comforting to the bereaved and the event can also provide them with the opportunity to meet staff who were involved with the dying person, which can have mutual benefits.

Support and care beyond the health service

Chaplains can make a significant contribution to the care of people who are bereaved through the effective use of their skills in supporting people and in utilizing their understanding of dying and death in the healthcare context, their ability to deal with issues of meaning, and their expertise in spiritual and religious matters. However, most bereaved people leave behind care settings, or services withdraw, and they face their bereavement not in the company of professionals but in the context of family, friends and the social networks provided in places of work, home and the communities with which they associate. Chaplains should therefore be aware of the resources of support and care that may be available to bereaved people once they have returned to the places in which their lives continue. It is also useful for chaplains to know how to access relevant advice and information about these resources and how a bereaved person may benefit from them.

Formal (paid) care of the bereaved may be provided through social care workers, including professionally qualified social workers. Bereavement can be a significant aspect of social care services either because service users have experienced loss in this way or there is need for social care input as a result of a death. However, much of the support available to bereaved people comes from voluntary and non-statutory organizations. One of the most well-known voluntary community services in the UK is provided by the national charity *Cruse Bereavement Care*, who offer support through a network of over 170 branches and 6,000 trained volunteers. Cruse offers free information and advice to anyone who has been affected by a death; provides support and counselling both one-to-one and in groups; offers education, support, information and publications to anyone supporting bereaved people; and increases public awareness of the needs of bereaved people through campaigning and information services.

Many national and local bereavement care resources have been established to meet the needs of specific groups. *Winston's Wish* is an example of a charity offering support throughout the UK to bereaved children and young people through a national telephone helpline, practical resources and publications, and a training and consultancy service for those working with bereaved families and those wishing to set up a grief support service in their own area. Another example is *The Way Foundation*, which provides a self-help social and support network to people bereaved under the age of 50 and their children. There are also many smaller and less permanent groups, often of a local nature, where people come together to share common experiences and to help others.

Bereaved people frequently come into contact with religious and cultural communities for the practical reason of arranging a funeral. These communities provide rituals, ceremonies and customs around death but many also offer some form of bereavement support. In Judaism, for example, the first seven days of intense mourning (*Shiva*) is a period in which the bereaved are exempt from the requirements of daily life, and the Jewish community demonstrate practical care and condolence in the provision of meals. In addition, there are Jewish support networks and counselling services. Christian churches, whose ministers conduct the majority of funerals, can provide pastoral care to bereaved people and there are

church-based bereavement visiting schemes offering community support through trained volunteers.

The virtual community of the internet provides access for
many people to a wealth of information and advice to help
them in their bereavement as well as a route to obtain support.
The style, quality and up-to-date nature of the content varies
widely. There are sites provided by statutory agencies, including the government's own online website, *ukonline.gov.uk*,
that contains a section on death and bereavement. In contrast,
there are sites developed from personal experiences that
many people will find helpful; *ifishoulddie.co.uk* was created
following the death of the author's father. The site provides
much practical information, including details about the legal
requirements following a death, organizing a funeral, and a
section on understanding and coping with grief. In addition to
published information and advice, the internet also enables
people with common bereavement interests to exchange personal experiences and information through discussion lists
and message boards. The internet also provides a place in
which to create virtual memorials for those who have died.

6

Different Faiths, Ethnicity and Culture

Hospitals are communities not defined by faith or culture but by illness and injury. Consequently, Christian chaplains have to be sensitive to the needs of other faiths, require knowledge of the major faith communities, and an understanding of the issues that may arise in the context of healthcare. This chapter aims to address this complex area by providing an approach to diversity and cultural competency. It is broken down in the following way:

- Identifying people: persons, patients and labels.
- Faith diversity.
- Chaplaincy in diversity.
- Cultural competence and spiritual sensitivity.
- Cultural competence in chaplaincy.

Identifying people: persons, patients and labels

Anyone who has been cared for in the NHS has been given a unique number that identifies the individual from all other healthcare users. One patient may share the same name as another patient, but the numeric identifier prevents any confusion and represents the distinctive healthcare record of an individual. However, individual patients share things in common: they may be of the same gender, they may be undergoing the same treatment, they may live in the same postal district.

People in general have these two characteristics: sameness

and distinctiveness. We associate or identify ourselves with other individuals who are similar to us in certain ways, and we distinguish ourselves from others whom we regard as different. In simple terms, identity is the way we determine how we are known by others and how others determine how they know us. Identity, therefore, can be understood as both a subjective and objective concept through which people understand their individuality in relationship to society.

The constitution of an identity involves multiple factors through which people choose to describe themselves and by which they are described or perceived by others. These factors intersect and interact with one another and may include: ethnicity; race; occupation; language; culture; religion; spirituality; gender; sexual orientation; skin colour; family and social relationships; health status; disability; heritage; and national origin. The many facets of identity are acquired, developed, negotiated and attributed through individual circumstances, experiences and social interactions. They inform and filter the self-understanding of individuals and modify the response of others to them. Inevitably, this interwoven texture of a person's identity is often reduced to a more basic level – for example, labelling someone as a patient. This form of stereotyping enables easy identification and predictability, but often at the expense of differences, variance and individuality. This can be illustrated by considering some of the popular attributions that might characterize patients: they are dependent upon and in need of the help of others; they are typically found in institutional settings, often in bed wearing nightclothes and identification wristbands; they are compliant with the instructions of healthcare professionals; and they receive tokens of concern from their family and friends.

A patient can therefore be distinguished from a healthy person: they can be located in particular places and they appear, behave and are treated differently. This is of course a crude description, but it is intended to illustrate how inherently simplistic conventional categories can be. Collective identities and stereotypes provide people with convenient terms that remove the need to negotiate and define every situation in particular detail. But categorizing people in this way obscures the subjective identity of individuals, assumes identity is inflexible and immutable, and raises critical questions about who determines what labels are applied, what they mean, and what consequences follow. The identity of an individual in a healthcare organization has often been determined by the latter with reference to a diagnosis or condition and through the clerking of simplified personal details. This approach obscures aspects of personhood that may relate to an individual's understanding and response to being unwell including beliefs and behaviours of a religious or spiritual nature. An uncritical and insensitive use of identifying labels referring to faith, belief and practice by health professionals may cause harm, inhibit healing and undermine necessary trust.

Faith diversity

The Census conducted in 2001 gave people for the first time the opportunity to register their religious identity. The statistics provide a rich source of data from which can be developed a snapshot of the religious landscape of Britain (Table 8). In summary, this shows that 72 per cent of the population identify themselves as Christian, 15 per cent declare they have no religion, and 5 per cent of the population identify themselves with other faith communities. This was a voluntary question, and 8 per cent of people chose not to answer it; however, from those that did, over 180 descriptors of religion were categorized. Religious pluralism is an evident feature of religion in Britain with its variety of faith communities. Some argue that growing pluralism undermines the plausibility of religion because their different propositions cannot all be 'true'. Others contend that the needs of a diverse society are reflected in religious variety, which is a sign of vitality. The reality is considerably less coherent and more nuanced, which is apparent in the disjunction for many people between the persistence of spiritual beliefs and a disassociation with

	Total population		Non-Christian religious population
	Numbers	%	%
Christian	41,014,811	71.82	n/a
Muslim	1,588,890	2.78	51.94
Hindu	558,342	0.98	18.25
Sikh	336,179	0.59	10.99
Jewish	267,373	0.47	8.74
Buddhist	149,157	0.26	4.88
Any other religion	159,167	0.28	5.20
No religion	8,596,488	15.05	n/a
Religion not stated	4,433,520	7.76	n/a

Sources: Census, April 2001, Office for National Statistics, General Register Office for Scotland, National Statistics website: *www.statistics.gov.uk*. Crown copyright material is reproduced with the permission of the Controller of HMSO.

Table 8   Population of Great Britain by religion (2001)

belonging to a faith community. But even within this broad demographic theme there are variations and contradictory examples, not least when people are admitted to hospital and face basic existential and spiritual challenges.

The relationship between self-identity, religious identity and group identity is problematic in terms of consistency and dependable assumptions. Starting with one aspect of a person's identity does not necessarily suggest others, but there are some aggregated characteristics that emerge when considering the population as a whole. By analysing information about the main faith groups, the Office for National Statistics presents features of religion in Britain that are relevant to healthcare services. For example, there are currently few older Muslim, Sikh and Hindu people (less than one in ten) in Britain, whereas one in five Jewish and Christian people are older people (aged over 65). Younger people (16–34 years) are more likely than older people to declare that they have no religious identity, and men more so than women. The rates of reported ill health and disability are highest for Muslims, with notable gender differences. However, the older age profiles of Christians and Jews mean that they have the highest proportions of people reporting ill health. Most Sikhs and Hindus are from an Indian ethnic background, three-quarters of Muslims are from an Asian background (43 per cent Pakistani, 16 per cent Bangladeshi), and Buddhism has the most ethnic diversity of any of the main religions (see Table 9).

The diversity of faiths in the population as a whole will be reflected differently at the local level of a hospital or health service where geographical and epidemiological factors will contribute to the variety of religions expressed by service users. Patient information collected by Trusts includes religion, and this data can be helpful in the provision and organization of chaplaincy services. However, questions asked of patients about their religion are voluntary; they may be omitted by the person asking the questions or incorrectly recorded. Religious data should therefore be used with care and the limits of its accuracy understood. A more meaningful interpretation of the data can be developed through gaining the perspective of the local faith communities who can contribute valuable expertise and understanding. In addition, staff also represent diverse religions and their views and needs should also be taken into account both in terms of their perspective on patient care and the provision of facilities and services for all people within the hospital or unit.

Chaplaincy in diversity

The health service aims to respect the diverse needs of patients and their carers and to treat them with dignity and respect. Responsiveness to individuals and equality of provision are principles that have a particular claim in the context of religious and cultural diversity. What this means for a chaplaincy

	Christian	Buddhist	Hindu	Jewish	Muslim	Sikh	Any other religion	No religion	Religion not stated	All people
White	75.7	0.1	0.0	0.5	0.4	0.0	0.3	15.3	7.7	100%
Mixed	52.5	0.7	0.9	0.5	9.7	0.4	0.6	23.3	11.5	100%
Indian	4.9	0.2	45.0	0.1	12.7	29.1	1.8	1.7	4.6	100%
Pakistani	1.1	0.0	0.1	0.1	92.0	0.1	0.0	0.5	6.2	100%
Bangladeshi	0.5	0.1	0.6	0.1	92.5	0.0	0.0	0.4	5.8	100%
Other Asian	13.4	4.9	26.8	0.3	37.3	6.2	0.9	3.4	6.8	100%
Black Caribbean	73.8	0.2	0.3	0.1	0.8	0.0	0.6	11.2	13.0	100%
Black African	68.9	0.1	0.2	0.1	20.0	0.1	0.2	2.3	8.1	100%
Other black	66.6	0.2	0.4	0.1	6.0	0.1	0.7	12.1	13.9	100%
Chinese	21.6	15.1	0.1	0.1	0.3	0.0	0.5	52.6	9.8	100%
Other ethnic group	33.0	15.5	1.3	1.1	25.7	1.0	0.9	14.1	7.5	100%

Source: Census, April 2001, National Statistics website: *www.statistics.gov.uk*
Crown copyright material is reproduced with the permission of the Controller of HMSO.

Table 9   Religion by ethnic group (percentage) in England & Wales (2001)

service will depend upon the representation of local populations within the hospital, but there are theological as well as
practical questions that need addressing to achieve these aims.
Chaplains cannot be all things to all people unless they are
prepared to either dissemble their own beliefs, values and faith
practice or abandon them to a lowest common spiritual
denominator. Conversely, the diversity that is afforded a
chaplain in the healthcare context presents opportunities for
discussion and collaboration based upon distinctive identities
that can enrich the care of patients and the culture of the
organization. At issue is how chaplains can exercise an
authentic ministry of care with integrity, but with an openness
and respectfulness for others.

The theological discipline of chaplaincy is one that makes
use of skills shared by a range of the humanities – for example,
philosophy, psychology and sociology. These various perspectives and methods give theology its richness and its ability to
engage with different experiences and contexts. What distinguishes the discipline of healthcare chaplaincy from the other
disciplines of humanity is that it has its own particular concerns and interests from which it has developed a specialized
knowledge. The field of enquiry for the discipline is one that is
circumscribed, at its simplest, by spirituality and the human
condition in the context of healthcare. But the scope of this
project overlaps with pursuit of others seeking to understand
illness and injury, and promote health and well-being. In this
sense, chaplaincy has a dialogical foundation that enables the
fruitful engagement of chaplains and ministers of religion
from distinctive traditions as well as the wider exchanges with
other healthcare professionals. Dialogue enables relationships, understanding and clarification; it encourages different
perspectives and it requires different voices. To put it another
way, this is a discursive process of contextual or practical
theology that enables a critical reflection on lived experience,
which for chaplains has a distinctively pastoral focus. Further,
the location of chaplaincy in the social context of healthcare
brings with it an invitation, if not an obligation, to dialogue,

which requires both a willingness to listen and the confidence to speak.

Chaplains stand on common ground with others by way of their createdness, their own frail humanity and their vocation to care. What they bring to the dialogue is their own experience and narrative derived from the stories of the individuals they have cared for and the stories of their own faith community. It is from this place that chaplains of one faith tradition may enter into an informed dialogue with those from different faith traditions in exploring questions of mutual concern and in considering an authentic pastoral response. Authenticity implies a particular rather than generic identity which can limit what a chaplain can provide in any specific situation. In addition, authenticity implies an awareness of the tacit values, beliefs, assumptions and frameworks that guide practice and behaviour and that distinguish different approaches to chaplaincy. It is from this awareness and particularity that chaplains from one faith tradition can engage with those in need from other faith traditions and create a space for caring dialogue and pastoral action.

The particular needs of the individual may require an understanding and a practice that are unknown to the particular chaplain or inauthentic to the chaplain's faith tradition. Equally, it is inconceivable that a chaplaincy department will contain the religious and spiritual variety present in the healthcare community. This is particularly evident for minority faith groups and those whose social structures do not contain existing roles analogous to a chaplain. Consequently, ensuring equitable provision in response to need is a demanding challenge for chaplaincy departments and one that requires a careful analysis of contributing factors within the hospital as well as those within the wider community. It also requires chaplaincy departments to be aware of their own prevailing service model and the values and beliefs that underpin it.

Cultural competence and spiritual sensitivity

Understanding patients as persons is fundamental to respecting their equal value and worth, but understanding persons in terms of their beliefs, values and behaviours enables specific care to be delivered that is relevant to and congruent with the individual's worldview. One size does not fit all when applied to healthcare services within a diverse context. What is required is both the individual capability and organizational capacity to be responsive to difference. This is increasingly referred to as *cultural competence*, a term that includes the ability of services to provide care relevant and sensitive to the religious and spiritual needs of different patients. Culture plays a critical role in the way people perceive illness, the beliefs they hold in respect to health and healing, and their attitudes and expectation towards healthcare providers.

Culture is also a feature of healthcare when considered as a group of people who have a set of common learned values and beliefs that are manifested in behaviour, social interactions and the interpretation of experience. The normative authority of the healthcare culture and its power in relationship to people who are unwell can easily eclipse the inherent culture of patients and their carers. This can be a very real barrier to comprehension and trust, which are essential in establishing a therapeutic relationship. Patients and their carers can also feel disrespected, unwelcome and unwanted. Consequently, patients may choose not to present with their healthcare needs or be treated ineffectively.

As an example of this cultural dissonance, consider the experience of people from the Deaf community whose distinct language, social customs, traditions, beliefs, values and history constitute a 'deaf culture'. The dominant medical culture in healthcare has generally defined deaf people in relationship to loss of hearing and disability. This pathological perspective understands hearing as normative, and therefore deaf people as impaired or disabled. This negative view may generate paternalistic and oppressive attitudes and behaviour towards deaf people that result in discrimination and disadvantage. In contrast, the Royal Association for Deaf People believes that deaf people are only disabled by the effects of social discrimination and exclusion. Deaf culture celebrates sign language as the first language of deaf people, whereas the dominant hearing culture may regard it as a stigma or a problem. In the Deaf community, sign language is an effective language system and deaf people seek to be recognized and valued as members of a linguistic minority group within society.

The first stage in developing cultural competence in healthcare requires a critical awareness of the cultural norms or dominant paradigms that operate within professions, services and organizations. Understanding the impact these norms have upon others, particularly those who are culturally different, will help to identify the barriers that inhibit effective cross-cultural working and sustain disparities in service provision. Developing the capacity to work with diversity will also require learning about different cultures and acquiring new skills and behaviours. In all this, the involvement of the different communities and their representatives will be vital; if not, there is a danger that services will resort to simplistic and misleading stereotypes. For example, it might be assumed that developing cultural competence in relation to deaf people is simply a matter of having staff that can use British Sign Language (BSL). But in working with deaf people, staff become aware of the greater role of touch in communication and that confidentiality is a visual as much as an aural issue in signed conversations.

Cultural competence in chaplaincy

Developing cultural competence and spiritual sensitivity in chaplains follows a similar path of self-awareness, learning and the acquisition of new skills and behaviours. For a chaplain, self-awareness is the foundation of effective practice and this is facilitated by reflective practice and supervision (see Chapter 2). This process enables the chaplain to evaluate how a particular situation was responded to and explore the assumptions on which it was based. A self-aware chaplain is not only able to understand the impact he or she makes as an individual on a situation, but is also mindful of unconsidered modes of thought and practice and capable of critiquing what may be assumed as self-evident. In developing self-awareness, chaplains will need to attend to their own biography, perspectives and worldview that constitute who they are as unique persons with distinctive identities. This self-understanding is often made more apparent when a chaplain is in an unfamiliar context or dealing with unknown cultural references. But from this dissonance, a chaplain will be more aware of his or her own limitations and barriers in providing care.

A key issue that will emerge in this process is to what extent differences matter and how far the boundaries of spiritual and religious care extend for the particular chaplain. It may be evident that a chaplain cannot practise religious ritual or interpret religious law and custom from a different faith tradition, but what are the limits, for example, of praying with someone or listening to what troubles them? In particular, a conflict of values or beliefs between the chaplain and the patient may present ethical problems in terms of how the chaplain responds, and potentially whether or not the chaplain can continue to offer care. For instance, pain and suffering can be understood as a test of faith or a consequence of former misdeeds. A patient with such beliefs may refuse pain-relieving medication and ask for the chaplain's support in persuading ward staff to leave them alone. If the chaplain's beliefs do not support this understanding of pain, there may be the opportunity to explore alternative courses of action or to consult with a representative from the patient's faith or cultural community. Even when the chaplain is unable to respond to the patient's request, care can still be offered and support made available. However, it should also be recognized that ethical or theological tensions may be irresolvable and that a chaplain may need to refer the patient to a colleague.

Self-awareness enables chaplains to engage more sensitively with the humanity of others in their uniqueness and in the ambiguity, uncertainty and tensions of pastoral encounters. It also makes chaplains more questioning of the assumptive world that we routinely operate in and more ready to be challenged. This process will disclose areas where lack of knowledge and understanding limits meaningful engagement with culturally different people and inhibits effective dialogue with people from a different religious or spiritual tradition. There is a wide range of resources available for chaplains to learn more about different cultural and religious traditions and these often provide general information that can be used as a guide. Subjects relevant to chaplains can include:

- Naming conventions.
- Gender roles and expectations.
- Personal space and touch.
- Language and patterns of conversation.
- Body language, gestures and facial expressions.
- Family and kinship structure, composition and authority, and their role in patient care.
- Community and religious structures and roles.
- Diet, cooking and dining traditions, and fasting customs.
- Religious observance and spiritual practices.
- Rituals and customs around major life transitions.
- Beliefs and practices related to health and illness.

Acquiring facts is the beginning of developing competency, which is learnt through practice. It is one thing to know that the first language of a deaf person might be BSL, it is quite another to develop a fluent level of signing. Patients and their carers can often be willing to teach chaplains about their culture or spirituality, but this raises ethical issues about the responsibility of the learner and the burden this may impose upon a patient. Instead, establishing links with leaders of other faith communities or representatives of cultural groups can prove mutually informative and lead the way to collaborative development work and supportive networks. Many healthcare organizations have resources devoted to promoting cultural competence and training staff; however, chaplains have a key role in terms of faith communities and are well placed to make connections with diverse communities.

The skills and behaviour of cultural competence for chaplains are principally aimed at respecting the integrity of persons from different cultures and to respond with sensitivity to the cultural dynamics of an encounter. Effective communication is a core skill, and in some situations a chaplain will not have the necessary linguistic competence and therefore will need to work with an accredited interpreter. An interpreter enables effective communication that is accurate and impartial; it is not the role of an interpreter to provide cultural advice or analysis. The linguistic needs of a patient should have been identified as part of an initial assessment, but this may not be the case for a patient's carers. In addition, patients or carers may have been assessed as having a sufficient level of English, but this may prove inadequate in stressful or challenging situations. Chaplains should know how to book an interpreter and what information is required. In working with an interpreter it is helpful to set aside time for a briefing prior to meeting a patient or carer. In the meeting the chaplain should face the patient or carer directly and address them in the first person, remembering that the interpreter is an aid to communication and not part of the discussion. However, sensitivity is required when discussing matters of a personal or intimate nature through a third party, and the gender and ethnicity of the interpreter should be considered.

As a service provider, a chaplaincy department will be expected to be responsive to the diversity of needs represented in the hospital community. This requires that departments understand the local nature of cultural diversity and the particular needs and requirements that this generates. Information can be obtained by analysing regional statistics as well as patient admission data and surveys undertaken in the hospital that include questions of culture, ethnicity and religion. From this information a department can develop its policies, structures and practices to ensure that they aim to respect diversity and enable cultural competency. This may involve reviewing different aspects of the department, including team membership, the type and use of facilities available for religious observance, the range of services offered, and the effectiveness of religious and cultural networks that chaplaincy is involved with or can access. Developing competency will also require identifying learning needs within the department and it may also disclose issues in other services that require addressing for chaplaincy to be effective. Throughout this process it is essential to involve and consult with actual or potential service users and representatives from their communities who can provide valuable and diverse perspectives, information and experience. Involvement of users and community representatives and a willingness for chaplaincy departments to learn can bring many mutual benefits and it can help foster effective partnerships necessary to address the needs of people from culturally diverse communities.

7

Non-clinical Work

Work with patients on the wards is underpinned and comple-
mented by a range of non-clinical tasks and activities that a
chaplain is required to undertake. This chapter provides a
basic introduction to what can be unfamiliar aspects of the
work and sets out suggestions to guide the inexperienced
chaplain. These aspects are:

- Being part of an effective chaplaincy department.
- Volunteers.
- Audit and service evaluation.
- Research.

Being part of an effective chaplaincy department

Chaplains rarely exist in isolation in healthcare and most will
be part of a department with other chaplains, volunteers and
administration staff. Consequently, chaplains will have to
deal with questions of how to work together and interact
effectively both as individuals and as a department as a whole.
Much of the clinical work of chaplains will be on a one-to-one
basis in which they may be considered part of a clinical care or
multidisciplinary team. However, the healthcare organization
will expect the chaplains' department to function effectively
as a professional and organizational unit, and in addition
chaplains will expect their departments to be a place of
support and sharing. A department in which members do not
get on with one another is going to be socially dysfunctional,
and a department in which members are unable to fulfil their

High task reflexivity

Cold Efficiency Team	Fully Functioning Team
• High task effectiveness	• High task effectiveness
• Average or poor mental health	• Good mental health
• Short-term viability	• Long-term viability

Low social   High social
reflexivity   reflexivity

Dysfunctional Team	Cosy Team
• Poor task effectiveness	• Poor task effectiveness
• Poor mental health	• Average mental health
• Very low team viability	• Short-term viability

Low task reflexivity

Source: M. West, *Effective Teamwork* (BPS Books, 1994).

Figure 7   Four extreme team types

tasks is going to be ineffective (see Figure 7). The task and social aspects of a department will impact upon the ability of the department to function effectively and for members to want to work together, stay together and develop.

A chaplaincy department needs a clear and shared vision of its orientation, values and purpose that is understood and supported by all members. The department's vision must relate to the organizational objects of the hospital and the needs of those who use the service. This vision must then be embodied in the aims of the department and the objectives and actions of each member. A well-functioning department requires effort and work by all its members who must recognize that they each have a responsibility for supporting the department and contributing to its effectiveness. Equally, a department needs to be structured and led in such a way that its members can participate and be involved in planning, problem-solving and decision-making.

Research supports the theory and experience that where there is clarity of tasks and objectives, clear leadership, high levels of integration, good communication and effective team processes, then a department has the conditions necessary to be well functioning and effective. This is demonstrated through meaningful interaction, high levels of participation, sharing of good-quality information, the capacity for critical reflection and creativity, learning together and mutual support. This requires effort, dedicated time, the commitment of members and their continuing development. It presents a particular challenge for departments with part-time members or small numbers of staff with staggered shifts. It may also test members of a department who wish to maintain the status quo and who employ defence mechanisms that inhibit effective teamwork. In the end it will rest with the departmental leader or manager to help members understand their responsibility to the department, to recognize the benefits of participating in the team and to organize and run departmental meetings and development sessions that promote interaction and involvement.

The work of chaplains is often demanding and an effective department can provide the support, communication, learning and leadership necessary to ensure valued, consistent and skilled spiritual care and pastoral practice. A good department will also recognize the different perspectives and approaches of members as an advantage in reflecting upon experience, analysing problems and working towards creative plans. This fosters a department's coherence, distinct identity and reputation, which can enable it to participate more effectively in a large and complex healthcare organization.

Volunteers

There is a long tradition of volunteering in health services, and chaplaincy departments provide excellent opportunities for people to volunteer for a range of roles including visiting patients on wards, accompanying patients to chapel services, and taking Holy Communion to patients. Volunteer schemes help people to participate in healthcare and find self-fulfilment in worthwhile roles. They also bring many benefits to chaplaincy departments and healthcare organizations and provide a valuable way of forging links with local faith communities, providing accessible support to patients and their carers, and increasing the reach and profile of chaplaincy within a hospital.

Volunteers play a significant role in the NHS and most Trusts have dedicated staff to organize and manage their volunteer programmes. A chaplaincy volunteer scheme should easily fit within the Trust's programme, while maintaining the distinctive nature of the volunteers required and the nature of their work. It is important therefore to identify the generic volunteer issues that can be dealt with by the Trust and what needs to be dealt with by the chaplaincy department (see Table 10). The starting point is to write a clear role description for each volunteer position that accounts for the tasks the volunteer will be expected to carry out, makes it clear how these complement and contribute to existing roles in the chaplaincy department, identifies how the department will provide support, and outline the training required for the role. The role description can be supplemented by a person profile that outlines the qualities and skills required to fulfil the role (see Table 11).

Recruiting and selecting suitable people for volunteer roles requires careful preparation and well-thought-through processes. The pastoral nature of the roles in chaplaincy has the potential to attract a range of people with a variety of motivations, some of whom will be seeking to work out their own needs more than they can meet the needs of patients. A good starting place is to hold an open event at which potential volunteer candidates can come to the chaplaincy department, meet some chaplains and any existing volunteers, hear about the role, the minimum requirements for applying, and ask any

	Trust (generic)	Chaplaincy (specific)
Recruitment	✓	
Selection and placement		✓
Occupational health screening and CRB checks	✓	
NHS induction and training	✓	
Chaplaincy induction and training		✓
Health and safety	✓	
Confidentiality		✓
Reimbursement of expenses	✓	
Support and supervision		✓
Discipline and grievance	✓	✓
Legal issues around volunteering	✓	
Rewards and recognition	✓	

Table 10 Responsibilities for volunteers in chaplaincy

questions. The selection process can then begin for those who apply to become volunteers. One approach, in this example for chaplaincy visitors, is to ask applicants to attend a foundation course in which they will learn about the role, the skills and behaviours required, and be asked to consider whether they think they are suitable candidates. The training programme also gives chaplains the opportunity to observe and work with candidates and to evaluate their suitability for the role. However, it needs to be made clear to candidates that the training is part of the selection process.

Following training, candidates are invited to attend an informal interview that provides them with the opportunity to explore what they learnt from the training, how they dealt with issues it raised, and whether they consider that they want to proceed with being a chaplaincy visitor. The interview allows this to be a mutual discussion with a chaplain to ensure that the decision is supported by both parties. It can be helpful if an existing volunteer is part of the interview to provide a

Outline chaplaincy visitor role description
- Regularly visit nominated wards.
- Make contact with patients and their visitors.
- Visit specific patients at the request of the chaplains.
- Provide social and pastoral support that respects the autonomy of individuals.
- Establish, deepen and end pastoral relationships with sensitivity, openness and respect.
- Pray with patients, their carers and visitors, when appropriate, and with their consent.
- Be ready to listen to and provide pastoral support to those who call at the chaplaincy department.
- Attend supervision and training sessions provided by the chaplaincy department.
- Attend mandatory training provided by the hospital.

Outline chaplaincy visitor person profile
- Function pastorally in a manner that respects the physical, emotional and spiritual boundaries of others.
- Be able to identify one's personal strengths and limitations in offering pastoral support.
- Respect diversity and differences, including – but not limited to – culture, gender, sexual orientation, spirituality and religion.
- Commended by their faith community for this role.
- Willing to learn and be able to reflect upon experience.
- Able and willing to commit a regular weekday time-slot.

Table 11   Sample role description and person profile for a chaplaincy visitor

different perspective. The candidates who have the agreement to proceed must then fulfil the requirements of the Trust's screening process which include references, an occupational health screen, and the disclosure of criminal records.

Unsuitable volunteers can easily bring a chaplaincy department into disrepute and jeopardize the effective work of chaplains; they can also be a potential hazard to patients. The effort put into recruitment and selection is therefore a worthwhile investment that the contribution of suitable volunteers far outweighs. The final stage is to place volunteers in suitable areas. Introducing volunteers into new areas requires careful preparation and consultation with staff. As a minimum, staff unfamiliar with chaplaincy volunteers should be briefed about their role, how they will be a benefit to patients and staff in a particular area, their lines of accountability and communication, and how they will be supervised. In the end, without the support of staff, volunteers cannot be placed in a particular area, but staff may also welcome the opportunity to have volunteers placed in their area and want to contribute to their training and support.

Audit and service evaluation

Chaplaincy departments are funded by the NHS to provide services that meet the needs of patients, their carers and staff. It is an expectation that services will meet certain standards and be of an acceptable quality. The quality of a service can be defined in a number of ways, but for health services it is generally understood to mean services that are achieving their intended benefit or outcome, acceptable to service users, equitable and accessible, and value for money. For example, in England all organizations providing NHS care will be expected to meet the level of quality described in *Standards for Better Health* to ensure that health services are provided that are safe; of an acceptable quality; are fair, personal and responsive to patients' needs and wishes; are provided equitably and that deliver improvements in the health and wellbeing of the population. The standards are organized within seven 'domains', which are designed to cover the full spectrum of healthcare:

1 Safety.
2 Clinical and cost effectiveness.
3 Governance.

4 Patient focus.
5 Accessible and responsive care.
6 Care environment and amenities.
7 Public health.

Applying these standards to chaplaincy means services that have (1) processes, practices and activities that prevent or reduce the risk of harm to patients (for example, chaplains receive fire safety training and know how to evacuate patients from their facilities), (2) chaplains who take account of any nationally agreed guidance, carry out their clinical care under supervision and leadership, update their skills and participate in regular clinical audit and reviews of their clinical services to ensure patients have their needs met, (3) leadership and systems of accountability and working practices to ensure probity, quality assurance, quality improvement and patient safety, (4) systems in place to ensure that care is provided in partnership with patients, their carers and relatives, respecting their diverse needs, preferences and choices, (5) care for patients that is prompt, with choice (for example, a Jewish patient may wish to see a Jewish chaplain), and without unnecessary delay at any stage, (6) environments that promote patient and staff well-being and respect for patients' needs and preferences, (7) collaborations with all relevant organizations and communities (for example, with local faith communities) and major incident plans.

Standards describe a level of quality that services are expected to meet or to aspire to and that they can be assessed against. Audit is the process by which care is systematically reviewed against predefined standards and where indicated changes are made to bring about improvements. The process of audit begins with identifying critical or sensitive aspects of a service and describing what best practice it should be achieving based upon research, guidelines, consensus and the involvement of users. From this, criteria are developed that describe an item or variable that can be measured as a proxy indicator of the level of quality being achieved. The actual measurement of the service against criteria requires data collection of some form and a representative sample is often used to make this exercise practical and feasible. Finally, data is analysed and from the results any necessary changes or improvements can be identified and implemented.

An example from chaplaincy concerns the response time of chaplains to urgent call-outs. In consultation with nursing and medical colleagues, it is decided that good practice should be for a chaplain to respond in 30 minutes from the time of the call to attending the patient in 85 per cent or more of cases. It is decided that for one month chaplains will maintain a separate log of all urgent call-outs that details the day and time the call is received and the time of attending, the ward requesting the call, the reason for making it, and the route they place the call. In addition, information is collected from the patient notes about the time the decision is made to call a chaplain. Data is collected over the chosen month and analysed. It reveals that delays occur where wards are unclear as to how to call a chaplain or who is responsible.

Consequently, a simple instruction sheet is prepared in consultation with switchboard staff about how to make an urgent call-out to the chaplain on duty and this is disseminated through a meeting with ward managers. The audit is repeated three months later and the criteria are achieved. What this example illustrates is the potential for audit to improve services, but it also demonstrates that audits need to be properly conducted and resourced and for this reason chaplaincy departments will benefit from involving clinical audit staff from within their organization.

Research

Think of research and most people think of laboratories, scientific discoveries and eminent professors claiming a major advance in knowledge. This is the high-profile end of research that makes newsworthy stories and reinforces the view that it is a small elite of professionals working in high-tech facilities who carry out research. It could not be farther away from the work of chaplains who deal with humanistic concerns, or sacred aspects of life, and the invisible and inscrutable nature of spirituality. Chaplains work with people, not test tubes; faith, not theories; and real events, not experiments. For these reasons it can be argued that research is irrelevant to much of what chaplains believe and practise. It requires skills that chaplains have not been trained in, resources that are generally not available to chaplains, and it appears to be a lot of effort for little result.

Chaplains do not work in isolation from the world; they seek to be responsive to those in need and make a difference to their spiritual well-being. In order to do the best they can for the people they minister to, chaplains require a reasonable understanding of the sort of problems that people face, their contexts, and how best to provide support and care that actually does good. Chaplains can develop a wealth of understanding and sensitivity to the dilemmas that people face through experience. But there are limits to what an individual chaplain can observe and be aware of, the first-person perspective can be incomplete or erroneous, and it is difficult to assess whether a well-intentioned action is helpful. For these reasons, a key skill for chaplains is the critical reflection and questioning that forms part of the practice of pastoral or practical theology. Informing this process should be a critical dialogue with the beliefs, traditions and practices of the chaplain's faith community as well as a rigorous analysis of particular pastoral experience. It is here that research can provide chaplains with a rigorous source of empirical knowledge and insights into human nature that can enhance critical reflection and the basis for pastoral action. If there is evidence that particular practice is not helpful or that it is potentially harmful, then chaplains have an ethical duty to change their practice in the light of this evidence. Research can also be a useful resource when reflecting on the nature and role of a chaplaincy service and the social context of pastoral care. It can provide data on the needs of a population, the demand

and use of a service, and the appropriateness or the effectiveness of a service.

The beginning of any research is a question that needs answering, for example, 'How effective is intercessory prayer for the alleviation of ill health?', 'Do patients benefit from attending a chapel service?' and 'How many patients are Buddhists in this hospital?' It might be that people have already considered the question and therefore searching the literature is always an important first step to find out if there already exists an answer. Research that duplicates other work unnecessarily or that is not of sufficient quality to contribute something useful to existing knowledge is considered unethical. Even when someone has published research into the question being considered it might be that the answer is inconclusive, the findings are not easy to apply, or there is a problem with the way the research was conducted. For example, a review of research assessing the effectiveness of intercessory prayer decided that the data was too inconclusive to uphold or refute the effect of prayer on healthcare outcomes. There were also methodological problems related to not knowing the exact nature, sincerity and duration of prayer and the extent to which extraneous prayer may have penetrated the intervention and control group. It can also be the case that relevant data is available but that it has not been examined to answer the question. For example, hospitals collect data about the religion of patients and this could be analysed to ascertain the numbers of patients admitted to the hospital over a defined period according to age and gender.

When there is nothing published or no existing data then there may be the basis for a research study. The research question and its associated aims will dictate the nature of study that needs to be undertaken. For example, a recent study in Scotland addressed the question, 'What do chaplains do?' The researchers chose a qualitative method that relied upon three data collection techniques: structured telephone interviews of 44 chaplains; case studies on three sites; and a second set of telephone interviews that pursued emerging themes. The data collected was analysed, and from the results a process model of chaplaincy was described. In contrast, studies designed to test whether prayer (or a treatment) is effective often make use of a randomized control trial in which patients are split into groups in a random way, with one group being subject to the treatment being tested and the other group (the control group) being subject to an alternative treatment (either of a different type or an inactive placebo). This allows researchers to compare the effects of the different treatments.

It will be evident that the basis of research is a systematic investigation that aims to contribute to existing knowledge by describing phenomena and developing explanatory theories. The systematic nature of a study using well-known techniques means that it is a transparent process that sets out the basis for data collection, how results are analysed and interpreted, and how conclusions are drawn. This methodological rigour means that a study should be capable of being duplicated and verified. But research studies have their limits and problems, and these are also written up in the literature and their consequences discussed. The assumptions and philosophy of research may also be problematic; for example, while systematic research aims to be objective and avoid bias, there are values inherent in the whole process – from the decisions of a funding body to those of journal editors. Finally, the limits of science impact upon research, particularly in relation to providing answers to the more profound questions of humanity and the nature and causes of human behaviour.

It is not unreasonable to expect that chaplaincy departments of a medium to large size should be engaged with research at some level (see Table 12). For instance, it should not be difficult for chaplains to establish a 'journal club' at which a chaplain presents a study from relevant published research for discussion. Building capacity for research in chaplaincy requires increasing the number of chaplains with knowledge of research principles and methods so that they can understand and be critical of the published research as well as contribute to and lead research studies. Many hospi-

Research awareness – the foundation level of research that all chaplains should consider developing. It involves accessing and reading the research of others, usually peer-reviewed published research in relevant fields. The next step on from this is to evaluate this research with a mind to informing practice.

Research participation – an intermediary level that draws upon research awareness. It can involve being an adviser to a research project, being responsible for parts of the research, or contributing to the fieldwork. In collaborating with others much experience can be gained.

Research innovation – designing research, writing a protocol, applying for funding and managing a project are some of the tasks involved in research innovation. Initiating and taking the lead in a research project is a demanding level. It requires significant research experience, knowledge of the field being studied, and a thorough understanding of research methodology and technique if the research is to be relevant, valid, reliable and ethical.

Table 12   Three levels of research

tals offer research courses to staff and there are many colleagues in other professions who are research-active and who are willing to help. Chaplains can also apply for local and national grants to fund research projects and provide the necessary resources for studies.

8

Professional Practice

The NHS demands that the disciplines that provide care for the sick are responsible, understand the ethical aspects of their work and act in the best interests of patients. In this chapter a framework is provided for professional practice that supports the responsibilities of the role and enables the chaplain to be accountable for practice. This is divided up into the following:

- Professional ethics and boundaries.
- Confidentiality.
- Consent and the disclosure of information.
- Chaplains and the Data Protection Act.
- Record-keeping.

Professional ethics and boundaries

Trust is the ethical bedrock for healthcare because it enables vulnerable people to place their well-being and lives in the hands of strangers. People looking for help and assistance with the impact of illness and injury on their lives need to be assured that they will be attended to, respected and not harmed. In straightforward and familiar situations, in which people have the opportunity to interact with one another in their daily lives, individuals can work out who they can trust. However, the context of healthcare for many people is an unfamiliar one that involves unknown people, practices and environments. Admission to a hospital dislocates individuals from many of the significant reference points in their lives and puts them in an organization with short-term interactions, structured relationships and elaborate routines.

This inherent difficulty in healthcare is overcome because patients have the proper expectation that healthcare professionals, despite being unknown, are trustworthy on the grounds that they pledge to promote and protect the good (health and well-being) of patients. The public promise of professionals must be demonstrated in practice and through every interaction with patients in order to establish and maintain trustworthiness. Establishing trust does not grant *carte blanche* permission for the professional to undertake any action. Trust is given to enable the professional to serve a particular good, but the patient retains the possibility of withdrawing this trust and refusing care. Professionals are obliged to honour the client's or patient's priorities and not to impose their own interests.

In the case of a chaplain and a patient, the grounds for trust are established between them because the chaplain's public office and promise is to serve the spiritual good or welfare of patients. A chaplain cannot serve a patient's spiritual good if that individual does not consider spiritual well-being a desirable good or has no interest in spiritual matters. The moral basis of the relationship requires a mutual interest in pursuing a particular spiritual good and this also sets the limits of the relationship. One way of describing these limits is to consider the boundaries within which chaplaincy functions, and that restricts what a chaplain may do in providing care and support. Chaplains are in positions of power and authority in relationship to those who seek their care and they have to deal with sacred and intimate aspects of people's lives. It is because chaplains believe in the value, worth and possibilities of being human that they are morally committed to refrain from harming the people they care for and are obliged to ensure that their personal encounters must operate within the parameters of disciplined, competent and accountable practice.

In any caring relationship there is always some element of ambivalence: that doing good may be doing harm, and that helping someone can easily be a cover for helping ourselves. The encounters that chaplains have with people also take place in hierarchical contexts in which there are clear differentials of power and authority. There is clearly much good that can be achieved when this power is exercised responsibly and for the benefit of those in need; and there is much harm and damage that can be caused when power is misused. Boundaries protect the vulnerable, provide guides to practitioners, and help maintain ethical expressions of power. One of the difficulties for chaplains is that their work is wide ranging and often relatively unstructured, informal and irregular. It usually proceeds without any explicit agreement, it takes place wherever there is need, and it is typically unplanned and reactive. The immediacy, flexibility and adaptability of chaplains can bring significant benefits to their work in the healthcare context, but it can also generate uncertainties and inappropriate expectations that can hinder spiritual care and pastoral support.

Chaplains should consider and assess the boundaries that guide their practice, enable them to be effective in the care they offer, and ensure that they act in the best interest of those they minister to. Making judgements about boundaries can be difficult when expectations are unclear, the situation is emotionally demanding or the chaplain is unable to critically reflect upon the situation. However, this framework for professional practice, while partly a matter of individual discretion, must also take into account a number of predetermined factors that include a chaplain's:

• moral commitments and beliefs;
• knowledge and understanding;
• skill and competency;
• constraints of time and place;
• professional code of conduct (see Chapter 12);
• relationship to any relevant law, policy and guidelines.

Establishing appropriate boundaries in the varied contexts of chaplaincy helps to clarify a chaplain's role and relationship with the person seeking care and support. Equally, they provide a reference for a chaplain to recognize practices, actions and types of relationship that are incompatible with ethical care and that are potentially or actually harmful. Chaplains therefore need to be confident in establishing the boundaries they consider are necessary and appropriate in any given situation. This may involve articulating to the person seeking care the reason for boundaries and clarifying the limitations that they impose. A chaplain may also need to negotiate with colleagues and other health professionals the parameters in which spiritual care and pastoral support can take place. Once established, however, boundaries at their best help to hold, frame and focus the fragile, intimate and sacred aspects of persons that chaplains are called to deal with and thus help create a safe and supportive space for care.

Confidentiality

In seeking to care for people who are ill and injured, healthcare professionals have to look beyond the pathology to the person as a whole and understand the particular context of the individual's life. Consequently, intrusive enquiries are not motivated by prurience or mere inquisitiveness, but the pursuit of information that is of potential assistance in providing care that benefits the patient. Information of this nature is necessary for good care and the assurance of confidentiality helps people to talk about personal, private and secret matters relevant to their health and well-being. Thus it can be argued that optimal care and benefit for patients requires a commitment to confidentiality. In addition to this consequentialist justification, the need for confidentiality in healthcare can be supported in terms of the ethical principles of autonomy and justice. A respect for autonomy implies that a patient's preference to maintain privacy limits the disclosure of information obtained about the individual. Justice dictates that patients have the right to control access to their own personal information and to have their confidences respected.

Staff employed by the NHS are contractually and ethically obliged to maintain confidentiality. However, confidentiality is rarely considered to be absolute, and while there is some protection in law for confidential information, there are also grounds for disclosure including: (1) the consent of the patient; (2) the public interest, particularly where there is a risk of harm; (3) the requirements of statutes such as information required for the investigation of crime. An absolute expression of a duty of confidentiality is in the formal act of confession when what a person says to a priest is considered to be secret. In the Roman Catholic Church the sacramental seal is understood to be inviolable, and a similar juridical and moral interpretation is found in the canon law tradition of the Anglican Church. It is clearly a deceit to assure patients that their personal information will be treated in confidence, but in reality disclose the information freely. This will only serve to undermine the trust essential to healthcare. Consequently, it is important to establish what the boundaries of confidentiality are, to inform patients of this before they disclose personal information, and to respect as far as possible the limitations of disclosure that an individual can reasonably expect or request.

Consent and the disclosure of information

Personal information is essential to providing good healthcare and chaplains cannot avoid handling patient information in some form when they are involved in patient care. The protection and use of patient information to support the delivery of healthcare is seen within the NHS as an important component of clinical governance and the quality of care. Compliance with confidentiality and security requirements within NHS organizations is overseen by the Caldicott Guardian, but anyone who obtains and makes use of patient-identifiable information must comply with the enforceable principles set out in the Data Protection Act (DPA 1998). The Information Commissioner has raised some important questions regarding the way that the NHS obtains and uses information from patients. In particular, the *NHS Code of Practice* (2003) recognizes that spiritual care cannot be practicably provided without access to some confidential patient information, but that before the information is disclosed to chaplains the explicit consent of patients is required.

The basis of consent is a respect for a person's self-determination and deliberate choice – in other words, autonomy. For consent to be valid or 'real' a patient must be competent to make his or her own decisions, voluntarily, and on the basis of adequate information. Respecting the self-determination of patients enables their genuine participation in decision-making and promotes their value as persons. Consent is not an action or a form-filling procedure, but a process that is about communication. Ethically significant consent requires that patients receive relevant and comprehensible information about the decision they are making as well as the possibility of refusal. However, while informed consent in theory is widely upheld as a necessary ideal, in reality healthcare relies upon consent based on a reasonable level of information and understanding because providing the fullest information for consent would impose severe practical difficulties in healthcare.

It is generally presumed that the presentation of a patient for healthcare, and the absence of a patient's refusal, implies consent to the sharing of personal information necessary to provide care. The basic demographic information collected by hospitals includes the religious affiliation of patients and this forms part of a patient's health record. It is self-evident that religious information will be of use to the professionals with the responsibility for meeting religious needs, hospital chaplains, in the same way that medical information will be of use to hospital doctors. Religious and spiritual information is not exempt from the ethical requirements of consent and patients should be able to retain discretion as to how much, and to whom, they disclose of their religious affiliations, spiritual beliefs and needs. Patients may choose not to offer any information of this nature, say upon admission to a hospital. This would not prevent a patient consulting with a chaplain, but it would be difficult to assess what – if any – care was needed without the willingness of that individual to discuss something of his or her spiritual orientation or religious affiliation.

Chaplains and the Data Protection Act

The first principle of the Data Protection Act (DPA 1998) requires that personal information is processed fairly and lawfully, which is satisfied by NHS bodies on the grounds that they are statutory bodies carrying out statutory functions in caring for patients who have consented to the use of the data. However, when using sensitive personal data (which includes information about the person's religious beliefs or other beliefs of a similar nature), at least one of an additional set of criteria must be satisfied. These include the explicit consent of patients and the processing of data necessary for medical purposes (which includes the provision of care) and is under-taken by (a) a health professional, or (b) a person who in the circumstances owes a duty of confidentiality which is equiva-lent to that which would arise if that person were a health professional.

The Office of the Information Commissioner has provided guidance on the use and disclosure of health data. The Information Commissioner considers that the disclosure of religious affiliation to chaplains is using data for a non-health purpose; a category similarly illustrated by disclosures of health data to the police and media. The guidance states that lawful processing of information about religious affiliation may be satisfied by obtaining the patient's explicit consent, or may in very limited circumstances be processed where it is necessary to protect the vital interests of the patient, but where consent cannot be given by the individual.

This guidance raises many more questions than it answers, and no explicit justification has been given for this position. However, the Information Commissioner assumes that the processing of health data by a health professional is subject to a duty of confidence and does not therefore require explicit consent. In addition, the Information Commissioner considers that acceptance of treatment by a patient implies consent to the use of data in the provision of care – for example, in routine record-keeping. Therefore, provided that these uses and disclosures are necessary to provide treatment in today's NHS, the Commissioner thinks that it is unlikely that a court would find that consent was invalid. Given that spiritual care is recognized in DoH guidance as an integral part of health-care, it is difficult to explain how the provision of care by NHS chaplains may be considered outside of the routine purposes of the NHS. In addition, while chaplains are not a statutory regulated health profession, the DPA makes provision for those who owe a duty of confidentiality that is equivalent to that which would arise if that person were a health pro-fessional. This duty of confidentiality is evident for chaplains in the professional Code of Conduct, the contractual obliga-tions of chaplains to their Trusts and the terms by which faith communities authorize chaplains.

The current situation for chaplains remains contentious and the majority of Trusts have taken a pragmatic approach that recognizes that simply withdrawing patient information from chaplains can be harmful to patient care, but that future developments in electronic record-keeping and care planning may enable patients to exercise a clearer choice in who has access to their information. The Information Commissioner has provided an interpretation of the DPA, but it is ultimately a matter for the courts to decide who will have to balance the confidentiality of patients with their right to manifest their religion or beliefs and to receive the care they require.

Record-keeping

Making and keeping records of patient care is established good practice for professionals working in the NHS and it fulfils a range of ethical and legal requirements. At their simplest, records provide chaplains with an *aide-mémoire* for continu-ing care and a log of their patient contacts. Chaplaincy records

> **A record is a tool to support good practice:**
> - Systematic account of care.
> - Framework for accurate information.
> - Means of effective communication.
> - Enable continuity.
> - Provide clear evidence for use in complaints and legal matters.
>
> **A record is a tool to develop practice:**
> - Personal professional development.
> - Service development.
> - Audit and clinical governance.
> - Research.
>
> ### Table 13   Purposes for chaplaincy records

can support good care practices because they are a consistent and effective method of recording the information necessary to plan and provide care to patients and their carers. In addition, they can provide a framework or set of prompts for the assessment of needs and they can facilitate good communication with patients, carers and colleagues. Chaplaincy records also have a number of secondary benefits, which include being a source of data on activity, providing a case summary that a chaplain can use in supervision, and being a record of the chaplain's actions and decisions should the case be subject to a complaint or court case (see Table 13).

When a patient is referred to a chaplain, either as a referral by a health professional or as a self-referral by the patient, a minimum set of information is required by a chaplain that needs recording (see Table 14). The chaplain should confirm before the consultation begins that the patient has requested to speak with a chaplain. In the event that the patient is not capable of consenting to the referral and disclosure of information – for example, because the patient is unconscious – disclosure may be justified on the grounds of necessity if it is clearly in the individual's interest and the disclosure is not

- Full name and ward/unit/location.
- Reason for referral.
- Urgency of referral.
- Religious affiliation.
- Necessary information to prevent harm to patient or chaplain.
- Information about any communication difficulties of the patient.

Table 14   Minimum information necessary for a referral to a chaplain

contrary to the individual's known values and beliefs. The views of people close to the patient, especially close relatives, partners and carers, about what the patient is likely to see as beneficial must be taken into account. The reasons for the referral should be documented in the record.

Patients should be told at the start of the consultation that chaplains keep confidential records of patient contacts as a matter of routine and the patient's consent should be obtained before proceeding. A patient may talk to the chaplain about highly sensitive and personal matters and these should be summarized with care and with regard to the confidentiality of third parties. In addition, a patient may indicate that the information may not be disclosed to anyone else. This should be respected unless there are clear grounds for disclosure in the public interest – for example, to prevent serious harm or prevent serious crime. However, in many cases it is helpful to the chaplain and acceptable to the patient to record in outline the nature of this sensitive information – for example, that the patient is under stress as a result of the breakdown of a significant relationship. A chaplain may also consider that all or part of this information may be helpful to the rest of the healthcare team in caring for the patient. In this example it would help the care team to understand why the patient is low in mood. The benefits of the disclosure should be discussed with the patient and disclosure should only be made with the patient's explicit consent, which should be documented.

It is best practice for chaplains to record their patient contact details as part of a multidisciplinary care record; however, this practice is limited and it is therefore more usual at present for chaplains to keep their own records. Chaplaincy records are best made on printed forms that have the approval of the Trust's Patient or Medical Record Committee (or equivalent) and are logged by the Trust's Caldicott Guardian and Data Protection Officer. The contents of a chaplaincy record may typically consist of three broad categories:

1 Information necessary to identify the patient and any established or pre-existing needs (e.g. name, religious observance).
2 Information associated with the current episode of care (e.g. ward, reasons for admission).
3 Information specific to the current referral to the chaplaincy team (e.g. reason for wanting to see a chaplain, assessment of need and planned care).

The record should summarize the contact with the chaplain in such a way that it can withstand two tests. First, any other chaplain should be able to read the summary, understand the nature of the referral, the care the chaplain offered, and any actions that needed to be taken. Second, the patient should be able to read the record, find no offence or disagreement with what has been written, and consider it a reasonable summary of the contact with the chaplain. Records should not contain personal views or opinions about the patient or the patient's carers. or visitors. There is no single model for a record; however, there are principles of record-keeping that have been adopted by health professionals and the NHS recommends best practice (see Table 15). In addition, a chaplaincy record may also make use of recognized coding that enables a chaplain to record succinctly the nature of the intervention (see Table 16).

Patient records should be:
- factual, consistent and accurate;
- written as soon as possible after an event has occurred, providing current information on the care and condition of the patient;
- written clearly, legibly and in such a manner that they cannot be erased;
- written so that any alterations or additions are dated, timed and signed in such a way that the original entry can still be read clearly;
- accurately dated, timed and signed or otherwise identified, with the name of the author being printed alongside the first entry;
- readable on any photocopies;
- written, wherever applicable, with the involvement of the patient or carer;
- clear, unambiguous (preferably concise) and written in terms that the patient can understand. Abbreviations, if used, should follow common conventions;
- consecutive;
- (for electronic records) using standard coding techniques and protocols;
- written so as to be compliant with the Race Relations Act and the Disability Discrimination Act.

relevant and useful in:
- identifying problems that have arisen and the action taken to rectify them;
- providing evidence of the care planned, the decisions made, the care delivered and the information shared;
- providing evidence of actions agreed with the patient (including consent to treatment and/or consent to disclose information).

and include:
- medical observations relevant to spiritual care;
- relevant disclosures by the patient – pertinent to understanding spiritual care needs or effecting care planned;
- facts presented to the patient;
- correspondence from the patient or other parties.

Table 15   Record-keeping best practice

Patient records should not include:
- unnecessary abbreviations or jargon;
- meaningless phrases, irrelevant speculation or offensive subjective statements;
- irrelevant personal opinions regarding the patient.

Source: Department of Health, *Confidentiality: NHS Code of Practice* amended (2003).

Table 15   Record-keeping best practice (cont.)

Pastoral assessment
An appraisal of the spiritual well-being, needs and resources of a person within the context of a pastoral encounter (ICD code: 96186-00; M-H 1824).

Pastoral ministry
The provision of the primary expression of the service (a 'ministry of presence' by 'being there'), which may include providing a ministry of presence, establishing of relationship/ engagement with another, hearing the story, and the enabling of pastoral conversation in which spiritual well-being and healing may be nurtured, and companioning persons confronted with profound human issues of death and dying, loss, meaning and aloneness (ICD code: 96187-00; M-H 1915).

Pastoral counselling and education
An expression of pastoral care that includes personal or familial counsel, ethical consultation, a facilitative review of one's spiritual journey and support in matters of religious belief or practice. The intervention expresses a level of service that may include counselling and catechesis, for example, and the following elements may be identified: 'emotional/ spiritual counsel', 'ethical consultation', 'religious counsel/ catechesis', 'spiritual review', 'death and dying' (ICD code: 96087-00; M-H 1869).

Table 16   Pastoral intervention codings

Pastoral ritual and worship
This intervention contains the pastoral expressions of informal prayer and ritual for individuals or small groups, and the public and more formal expressions of worship, including Eucharist and other services, for faith communities and others. Elements of this intervention include (a) 'private prayer and devotion', bedside 'Communion' and 'Anointing' services, 'Blessing and Naming' services for the stillborn and miscarried, and other 'sacrament' and ritual expressions; (b) 'public ministry', 'Eucharist/Ministry of the Word', funerals, memorials, seasonal and occasional services (ICD code: 96109-01; M-H 1873).

Sources: The World Health Organization, International Classification of Diseases (ICD), Volume 10, Australian Modification (AM) Pastoral Interventions; *http://vic.uca.org.au/AHWCA/*; Website of the Australian Health & Welfare Chaplains Association (AHWCA).

Table 16   Pastoral intervention codings (cont.)

Records should be made promptly. A contemporaneous record is more likely to be an accurate reflection of actual events, rather than an interpretation with the benefit of hindsight. Retrospective documentation may suggest that a course of action was based on dubious reasoning, or needs extensive justification. It is also important that records show clearly the reasoning behind any decisions made by the chaplain or the process by which a patient makes a significant choice – for example, why bereaved parents decide to choose the burial of their deceased baby. Documenting thought-processes and decision-making not only benefits chaplains using the records in the future, it also protects them in cases of complaints or litigation. If after the contemporaneous note has been made it becomes clear that more information should have been included, a fresh entry should be made, dated accordingly, with an explanation of why additional information is now considered necessary.

In order to maintain patient confidentiality, it is important that written records are stored securely within an office and filed so that the record can be found easily if needed urgently. Electronic records need to be held on a secure password-protected NHS network. Chaplaincy records should always be inaccessible to members of the public, and not left even for short periods where they might be looked at by unauthorized persons. Patients have a right to apply for access to their records and obtain copies of them. Chaplaincy departments therefore need to log the records they hold, have a clear process to differentiate active from closed records, and follow NHS guidelines for their retention and disposal.

9

Ritual and Liturgy

Chaplains are frequently called upon to perform a variety of liturgical duties – from saying a prayer with an anxious patient, conducting a funeral for a non-viable foetus, through to dedicating a window in memory of a member of staff. There are few ready-made prayers or rites for these occasions and this chapter provides some useful resources for use by chaplains in a range of situations, as well as considering chapel services:

- The role of ritual and liturgy in healthcare.
- Prayer and blessings.
- Confession and reconciliation.
- Laying on of hands and anointing the sick.
- Holy Communion.
- Emergency baptism.
- Affirmation of relationships and marriage.
- Commendation at the end of life.
- Commendation and naming of a dead baby.

The role of ritual and liturgy in healthcare

If healthcare is about attending to suffering and working towards healing, then liturgy and ritual have much to contribute. Liturgy can be the means of articulating our desire to be whole; and ritual can be a framework in which people make sense of the losses and wounds acquired in living and dying. Through them, we can express something of human dignity and worth before God and recognize something of the gracious mystery of being human. Both may also challenge and disturb because they can create the space in which we confront truths we dare to speak or glimpse the people we dare not imagine we are called to be. The words and actions of liturgy and ritual create an environment of meaning that can nourish and restore. They can contain the unbearable, express the unimaginable, and point us beyond the mundane towards the Holy. Therefore liturgy at its best deals with the ambiguities, and ritual holds in tension the contradictions experienced in life and death.

The chaplain is unique among health professionals in providing religious rituals, many of which draw upon the rich traditions of Christian communities. However, the use of these traditions needs shaping by the pastoral circumstances to which they are brought. This requires that liturgy is part of the dialogue of the pastoral encounter and is itself a means of care. Ritual and liturgy provide a place for telling our stories and retelling the story of Christ. Liturgy is therefore incarnational: it takes place within space and time; it is embodied in the spoken word and gesture; it is made tangible in touch and symbol; and it can embrace individuals within the body of Christ. Liturgy and ritual are most effective therefore when they incorporate people and make real something of the intangible. This finds its fullest meaning in the sacraments, through which people participate in God's grace, and by which people encounter life in all its fullness.

Liturgy is never ordinary, informal or makeshift, but prepared, ordered and patterned following the traditions of the Christian community in order to celebrate the work of God. When people are perplexed or feeling insecure and uncertain, this may be compounded by liturgy that is unstructured, tentative or haphazard. None of this excludes the freedom and flexibility required in pastoral situations to reflect what is happening and to incorporate what is significant at that moment. Equally, ritual should not be pretentious, obscure or ceremonial for its own sake. But liturgy and ritual in the service of people in demanding pastoral circumstances should be confident, reassuring and caring. In all this, liturgy relies heavily upon the language of word, symbol and gesture to communicate clearly. These all need careful thought and a reliable approach; they also require us to be in tune with the people we are with. While language by its nature is limited in its precision this is no excuse for clumsy and insensitive language either about the situation we are addressing or God. Rather, liturgy and ritual in a health setting should be alert to the problematic aspects of some religious metaphors, images and symbols, and aware of the creative possibilities that the rich and living Christian tradition offers.

Before beginning any liturgy or ritual, it can be most helpful and reassuring to explain clearly and simply what will be happening. This is particularly important in an anxious situation or where people are unfamiliar with the form of liturgy being used. For example, before distributing Holy Communion to a patient for the first time, an explanation will remove the uncertainty of an unfamiliar form of liturgy. In particular, it helps to tell people which parts they will be expected to join in with and how a sacrament will be administered. Be prepared to guide people through a service, be ready to shorten liturgy for those who find it hard to concentrate or stay awake for whatever reason, and be able to hold silence when it is simply inappropriate to impose liturgy or ritual on a situation that cannot bear it.

In what follows, particular pastoral situations will be presented from a liturgical perspective and illustrated with liturgical examples. This is not an exhaustive selection, but one that covers some common pastoral situations with the aim of demonstrating liturgical principles and providing ideas and inspiration. Chaplains generally operate under some form of ecclesiastical licence or authority, and this may prescribe the liturgies that can be used. However, there is usually latitude among the rubrics to adapt official liturgies to circumstances or to make use of alternative material. Chaplains may also face situations that have no associated authorized liturgy, in which case an understanding of liturgical syntax and the structures of ritual will be a guide. Whatever the case, chaplains need to maintain their knowledge of liturgical developments and maintain a library of resources.

Prayers and blessings

Common prayer is part of the heritage of the Church, but many individuals turn to prayer in times of need whatever their relationship to the Church. Prayer is a basic spiritual practice that enables people to pause before God and be mindful of the divine presence. Prayer can be expressed in words and action as well as in silence and stillness; it may be patterned on the offices and devotional practices of the Church, or it may be non-liturgical and wrought out of immediate experience. There are many reasons why people pray in hospitals, and for these same reasons people may abandon prayer. Through prayer people may therefore come to address God out of hope, despair, repentance, protest, gratitude and for many other reasons. And if people face God in prayer, then it turns them towards divine love and truth, which are awesome, comforting, challenging and liberating.

Prayer requires attention and focus, both of which can be difficult in the environment of a hospital and when a person is suffering. However, when someone wants to pray they can be supported by praying with others and in using familiar forms of prayer. People may be too ill to pray or welcome the offer of prayer from a chaplain; this brings with it the challenge of the subject and content of prayer. As with other aspects of pastoral care, there is a danger in praying that a situation is misunderstood or exaggerated. Prayer should be based in the reality of the encounter and should not include speculation. It can therefore be helpful to ask a patient or those at the bedside what they might want to be included in prayer. Finally, prayer should be grounded in ethical practice and should never be used as a form of preaching, to cover an awkward moment, or to curtail a difficult visit.

If liturgy is understood as faith in action, then a blessing may be considered as an action of thanksgiving and sanctifying that articulates a belief in God-with-us. Blessings are familiar to many as the concluding element of a liturgical rite, but a blessing can also be used as a distinct liturgical action. In the Christian tradition both people and objects have been blessed, and in so doing the Christian community has boldly affirmed something of the goodness of the material and created order. A blessing is thus the assertion that God's grace comes through the world and affirms God's engagement with the real and actual.

In healthcare, people are obvious candidates for blessing, but there are many representative objects that are significant to people that may also become the subject of a blessing. These include tokens of relationships, symbols of faith and memorials. Whatever is being blessed, it is important to be aware of the context out of which a request for a blessing comes and to acknowledge this in the liturgy. Blessings frequently mark moments of change, such as the dismissal from the liturgical assembly, or at an important stage in someone's journey, and this may shape the form of the liturgy. The sign of a cross is commonly used in an act of blessing, but water, the laying on of hands and other actions can be incorporated in a liturgical blessing.

A Service for Blessing a Memorial Window is on page 162

Emergency baptism

When a person, adult or infant, has not been previously baptized and where there is doubt that the person will recover from their illness or injuries, a chaplain may be called upon to perform a baptism. A request for baptism can be motivated by a mix of reasons in a hospital, as it can in a church. Social etiquette, family pressures or simply the opportunity to do something in a desperate situation are but a few of the common reasons. Baptism is an encounter with ambiguity and this is reflected in the central symbol of the rite. Water contains contradictions of life and death, anxiety and pleasure, hope and despair, threat and promise. These are the often unconscious and irrational struggles that present themselves to a chaplain when a request for a baptism is made in an urgent way.

Baptism is the sacrament by which people are incorporated into the Christian Church and it is commonly subject to some form of discrimination. There may be a tension, therefore, for the chaplain in desiring to respond to a pastoral need while wanting to maintain an ecclesiastical integrity. However, responding with respect to the request must be the starting point that can lead into a more thorough exploration of what lies behind it. Powerlessness is often a significant reason for a request in a healthcare setting, where people are cared for but to the exclusion of those who love them. Baptism may therefore be a deeply caring act that can embody both human and divine aspects of love. Through a rite of baptism, a person is honoured and identified as a uniquely valued child of God in a situation where illness and the technology of care may easily obscure the person.

Baptism, as an act of the Church, is a constant reminder that we are members of a diverse community of the living and dying, the weak and strong, the young and the old, in which all are cherished by God. Baptism is also a tangible means of God's grace that is offered out of a forgiving and empowering love and marks the beginning of new life in Christ. If the patient recovers, it is proper for the chaplain – with the person's consent or, if a minor, the consent of the parents – to refer the person on to a suitable church where they can be received and continue in the journey of faith.

Baptism rites can be adapted to suit the circumstances and it is clearly inappropriate in a healthcare setting, particularly in an urgent situation, to follow an extended liturgy intended for a celebration in church. As a minimum, most churches accept the administration of water in the name of the Father, the Son and the Holy Spirit (Matthew 28.19). It is also permissible that a lay person may be the minister of baptism. Additional elements of baptism may be included, although lighted candles must not be used in places where medical oxygen is present. For Roman Catholics, confirmation, administered by a priest, may follow baptism as part of the sacraments of Christian initiation.

Baptism, as a sacrament, is the means of conveying God's grace to the living who participate in the community of Christ. There is no theological justification for baptizing the dead, and in pastoral terms it contradicts the reality of what has happened. There is no need for apology when this issue arises because the chaplain is not left without any response, for death is accompanied by its own distinctive liturgy. When a request has been made for a dead baby to be baptized, this response can include some form of name-giving liturgy in addition to a commendation. What is helpful in all these circumstances is for staff to know and understand what the practice of the chaplaincy department is in order to provide accurate information.

A Service of Baptism for a Baby Who Is Critically Ill or Injured is on pages 163–5

Confession and reconciliation

Individual confession and reconciliation is subject to a wide variety of interpretations, meaning and practice. What is common is the need for people to address the things that alienate them from God and from others, to resolve conflicts, and to find forgiveness and peace. For some, confession will be part of their Christian discipline and will follow a clear format. For others, the challenge of illness may prompt them to evaluate and consider their lives afresh. This can give rise to the need to acknowledge the truth about burdensome aspects of their lives that they now want to deal with in a desire for wholeness and healing.

People can avoid the truth and responsibility they have for their sins of commission and omission. But being able to name actual wrongs and to declare that which has been hidden or denied can be a liberating task. People therefore may need guidance and support in self-examination and in making a confession. It is important also that people are assured of the confidential boundaries within which a confession will take place (see Chapter 8). However, chaplains should avoid switching into confessional mode at the first hint of contrition. People can develop an erroneous sense of guilt or they may have a negative sense of themselves that results in feelings of shame. In such situations an act of confession and reconciliation is unlikely to resolve the underlying difficulties and the chaplain needs to be able to discern and discuss what may be the appropriate response. In a healthcare setting, the chaplain needs to be sensitive to damaging moral subtexts that relate ill health to sin and be aware of prejudices and values associated with particular conditions.

Whether a formal or informal mode of confession is used, it is important that a clear pronouncement of forgiveness is made. If the absolution is vague or hinted at, then the person weighed down by guilt will remain unsure of their reconciliation and uncertain of how much God has accepted their repentance. The chaplain is not acting as judge, but as pastor of those burdened and entangled by sin. Therefore absolution should not be reserved as a reward for the exceptional efforts of the few, but used with compassion as an unequivocal sign of God's grace freely given.

A Service for Confession and Reconciliation is on pages 166–7

Laying on of hands and anointing the sick

The use of the laying on of hands and anointing with oil are liturgical actions found in a number of forms in Christian worship. In the context of the pastoral care of the sick, these are actions of the sacramental community of the Church that express in a visible and embodied form God's grace and blessing. Both are actions involving touch, a basic human gesture that can communicate reassurance, affirmation and love. The haptic sense develops before sight and language, and it is fundamental to human experience and connecting with others. But touch is not value-free; it is conditioned by social norms and it can convey powerful signals. Therefore touch may be perceived as threatening or manipulative; it could be physically painful and it can be a form of abuse. In the hospital context, touch of any form needs careful consideration and an awareness of the ethical issues.

The association of certain oils with healthcare is something both ancient and contemporary. In the Christian tradition anointing of the sick with oil is recorded in the New Testament (Mark 6.13; James 5.14–15) and rites exist in a number of traditions. As a sacramental action, anointing is often subject to church discipline and order, with restrictions on who may bless the oil and use it for anointing. In addition, there are practical issues to be considered. Oil is not sterile and it can be messy. Oil stocks are available to convey oil and it is sensible to have a supply of tissues available. An assessment of the patient's skin integrity and vulnerability to infection will need to be considered for some patients.

A Service for the Laying on of Hands and Anointing the Sick is on pages 168–9

Distribution of Holy Communion

Many patients in acute wards are unable to attend a hospital chapel for a celebration of Holy Communion. People who are regular communicants may require your support in maintaining this practice and others may be glad to be offered the opportunity to receive Holy Communion as a source of strength and healing. However, when people are ill, the thought of receiving Holy Communion may be difficult because of nausea or pain or exhaustion. It can also be the case that people feel less than worthy in their present state and condition to receive, and some may consider that a busy hospital ward in which they are not properly dressed is hardly a fitting place in which to administer a sacrament. Clearly, there is a need to provide the patient with the opportunity to discuss these matters and to ensure that this person is properly prepared for receiving Holy Communion. The patient's visitors may also need considering, and it may be necessary to schedule the service so that others significant to the patient can be present.

The pastoral context cannot be considered in isolation of the clinical context. Account should be taken of relevant risks for the patient, and in particular their mouth condition, swallow reflex, gluten sensitivity and vulnerability to infection. A patient may not always think of telling a chaplain about these things, and therefore you need to check with a nurse if there are any reasons why a patient should not receive Holy Communion. It may also be necessary to consult with a doctor, dietician or speech and language therapist about a particular patient. Finally, in addition to clinical risks, there are the more usual hazards on the ward that need avoiding if Communion is to be uninterrupted – such as the patient being taken off for an X-ray or being already timetabled for some therapy.

The practice of distributing Holy Communion is both a practical and liturgical matter. Practically there is the matter of what form and how consecrated bread and wine are going to be transported to the bedside in such a way that is safe, hygienic and dignified. If wine is to be conveyed, this needs to be done securely and a used chalice or cup will need to be dealt with. Alternatively, wafers can be intincted before distribution on the wards. Liturgically, people need to feel secure enough with the rite being used so that they are not anxious and wondering what is coming next. A common rite for all patients may be an ecumenical ideal, but at a time of uncertainty a familiar pattern or prayer may be enormously helpful and reassuring.

A Service for Distribution of Holy Communion in Hospital is on pages 170–3

Affirmation of relationships, marriage and civil partnerships

The meaning and value of relationships can often come into focus when a person is dislocated from the people who usually provide companionship, nurture and support. For some this may give rise to a desire to celebrate a relationship or to make a deeper commitment to it. These acts of affirmation bear witness to the power and beauty of love, and therefore of God. This means that we are approaching something mysterious, unbounded and sacramental. And because relationships are embodied, it also requires us to acknowledge dimensions that are emotional, physical and sexual. Human relationships exist on a broader spectrum than most official liturgies acknowledge, and it is therefore a privilege and a challenge for a chaplain to be called upon to celebrate the varied ways in which people are drawn to one another in friendship and love.

Two people may seek to obtain legal recognition of their relationship while they are in hospital and chaplains are often involved. Lesbian and gay couples can form a civil partnership and opposite-sex couples can opt for a religious or civil marriage ceremony. A civil partnership or marriage can usually take place in hospital when a patient, according to the opinion of his or her doctor, is seriously ill and not expected to recover, cannot be moved to an approved venue, and understands the nature and purport of a civil partnership or marriage. The Registrar General can authorize at short notice civil partnerships and marriages by civil ceremony and by religious ceremony other than in the Church of England or Church of Wales. Marriage in hospital according to the rites of the Church of England can be authorized by an Archbishop's special licence. The local Registrar's Office and the Faculty Office of the Archbishop of Canterbury will give advice and guidance and should be approached at the earliest stages of preparations. There may be a considerable degree of uncertainty about the patient's condition, which may change rapidly or unpredictably – and consequently so may the person's capacity to consent. This should be taken into account when planning the event and all concerned parties should be made aware of the situation.

A Service for Affirmation of Relationships and Marriage is on pages 174–7

Commendation at the end of life

The final stage of a person's life and the approach of death may be a time in which those present may want to set this mortal human event in a wider spiritual context. Although there is an obvious certainty in death and an unavoidable parting, there is also ambiguity and a sense of going forth. In liturgy these can be honestly named, and through ritual they can be expressed in ways that may be helpful and hopeful. But because liturgy can be powerful, it is crucial that a chaplain is fully informed of the condition of the patient and does not enter into a situation unaware of what is understood by those present. It is irresponsible to perform a commendation based on assumptions. However, even where there is no doubt that the patient is dying, it may be many days before the end of life. Therefore careful consideration should be given to the pastoral needs of the patient's carers that is informed by an understanding of the dying process.

A commendation at the end of a person's life can take a number of forms, from a simple recitation of the *Nunc dimittis* through to an extensive rite. Commending the dying to God can span acts of remembrance, thanksgiving, forgiveness, communion, affirmation and blessing. A commendation by a Christian chaplain can also be an act of hope in that it can point people beyond the immediate reality of death towards the resurrection promise. The shape and form of the commendation will depend upon the patient's beliefs, practice and condition. When a patient is unable to communicate his or her own needs, a chaplain will need to rely upon any prior knowledge, available information and the views of those close to the patient. The aim is to provide what is best for the patient and this may require some discussion and negotiation. It is helpful to explain what form the commendation will take and to give permission for people who do not wish to be present to step out for this period.

A Service for Commendation at the End of Life is on pages 178–80

Naming and commendation of a dead baby

The death of a baby before or around the time of birth can be a devastating experience. Parents preparing to welcome new life into their family are faced with death and the need to say goodbye. But people differ as to what they are saying goodbye to, and this depends upon how they might answer the question of when the human individual should be thought to exist. For some, conception marks the beginning of the person and the embryo is considered to be the early stages of an unborn child or baby. Some may consider that the foetus has the potential to develop into a person, but that the emerging life must reach sustainability outside of the womb to be thought of as a baby. These moral dimensions are equally present when a pregnancy has been terminated and parents have to face similar questions.

Whatever the cause of the end of the pregnancy, parents

may wish to have the opportunity to have their baby commended to God. They may also wish to recognize that this emerging life was not no one, but someone precious who was gaining a place in their lives and who was known more and more as an individual. For this reason, naming and commending liturgies may provide an appropriate ritual to enable parents to acknowledge the life that was coming into being and to express loss and grief. A ritual act may also be a memorable occasion that enables parents to express their love and care for their expected child. If a naming takes place it can be helpful to provide some form of naming certificate that marks the occasion and provides one of few mementos of a short and hidden life.

**A Service for Naming and Commendation of a Dead Baby
is on pages 181–3**

10

Bibliography and Further Reading

Introduction

Cox, J. G. (ed.) (1955), *A Priest's Work in Hospital: A Handbook for Hospital Chaplains and Others of the Clergy Who Visit Hospitals*. London: SPCK.

Department of Health (2003), *NHS Chaplaincy: Meeting the Religious and Spiritual Needs of Patients and Staff*. London: Department of Health.

Mowat, H., Swinton, J., Guest, C. and Grant, L. (2005), *What Do Chaplains Do? The Role of the Chaplain in Meeting the Spiritual Needs of Patients*. Aberdeen: Mowat Research.

Orchard, H. (2000), *Hospital Chaplaincy: Modern, Dependable?* Sheffield: Sheffield Academic Press/Lincoln Theological Institute.

SEHD (2002), *Guidelines on Chaplaincy and Spiritual Care in the NHS in Scotland*. Edinburgh: Scottish Executive Health Department.

SYWDC (2003), *Caring for the Spirit: A Strategy for the Chaplaincy and Spiritual Healthcare Workforce*. Sheffield: South Yorkshire Workforce Development Confederation.

1   The Context of the NHS

History

Brunton, D. (ed.) (2004), *Medicine Transformed: Health, Disease and Society in Europe 1800–1930.* Manchester: Manchester University Press.

Cherry, S. (1996), *Medical Services and the Hospital in Britain, 1860–1939.* Cambridge: Cambridge University Press.

Elmer, P. and Grell, O. P. (2003), *Health, Disease and Society in Europe 1500–1800: A Sourcebook.* Manchester: Manchester University Press.

Granshaw, L. and Porter, R. (eds) (1989), *Hospitals in History.* London: Routledge.

Orme, N. and Webster, M. (1995) *The English Hospital 1070–1570.* Yale: Yale University Press.

Rawcliffe, C. (1999), *Medicine for the Soul: The Life, Death and Resurrection of an English Medieval Hospital.* Stroud: Sutton Publishing.

Risse, G. B. (1999), *Mending Bodies, Saving Souls: A History of Hospitals.* New York: Oxford University Press.

Smith, L. D. (1999), *Cure, Comfort and Safe Custody: Public Lunatic Asylums in Early Nineteenth-century England.* Leicester: Leicester University Press/Continuum.

The NHS

Binleys (2005), *Binleys Guide to the NHS.* London: Beechwood House Publishing.

Department of Health (1997), *The New NHS: Modern – Dependable.* London: HMSO.

Department of Health (2000), *The NHS Plan.* London: Department of Health.

Department of Health (2001), *Shifting the Balance of Power*. London: Department of Health.

Department of Health (2005), *Department of Health: Departmental Report 2005*. London: Department of Health.

Harrison, A. and Dixon, J. (2000), *The NHS: Facing the Future*. London: King's Fund.

Levitt, R., Wall, A. and Appleby, J. (1999), *The Reorganized National Health Service*. Cheltenham: Stanley Thornes (6th edition).

NHS Confederation (2003), *The NHS in England 2003/4*. London: NHS Confederation.

Office for National Statistics (2003), *UK 2004: The Official Yearbook of the United Kingdom of Great Britain and Northern Ireland*. London: HMSO.

Porter, R. (1997), *The Greatest Benefit to Mankind*. London: HarperCollins.

Rivett, G. (1998), *From Cradle to Grave: Fifty Years of the NHS*. London: King's Fund.

Scottish Executive (2003), *Partnership for Care: Scotland's Health White Paper*. Edinburgh: Scottish Executive Health Department.

2   Being a Hospital Chaplain

Campbell, A. V. (1986), *Rediscovering Pastoral Care*. London: DLT (2nd edition).

Cobb, M. and Robshaw, V. (1998), *The Spiritual Challenge of Health Care*. Edinburgh: Churchill Livingstone.

Department of Health (2004), *Knowledge and Skills Framework*. London: Department of Health.

Gerkin, C. V. (1997) *An Introduction to Pastoral Care*. Nashville: Abingdon.

Goodliff, P. (1998) *Care in a Confused Climate: Pastoral Care and Postmodern Culture.* London: DLT.

Hawkins, P. and Shohet, R. (2000), *Supervision in the Helping Professions.* Buckinghamshire: Open University Press.

Kerry, M. (2001), 'Towards Competence: A Narrative and Framework for Spiritual Care Givers', in Orchard, H. (ed.), *Spirituality in Health Care Contexts.* London: Jessica Kingsley.

Lyall, D. (2001), *The Integrity of Pastoral Care.* London: SPCK.

Pattison, S. (1989), *Alive and Kicking: Towards a Practical Theology of Illness and Healing.* London: SCM.

Pattison, S. (2000), *A Critique of Pastoral Care.* London: SCM (3rd edition).

Speck, P. (1988), *Being There: Pastoral Care in Time of Illness.* London: SPCK.

VandeCreek, L. and Burton, L. (eds) (2001), *Professional Chaplaincy: Its Role and Importance in Healthcare.* Decatur, Georgia: Association for Clinical Pastoral Education.

Webster, A. (2002), *Wellbeing.* London: SCM.

3   Clinical Work

Bruce, S. (1996), *Religion in the Modern World.* Oxford: Oxford University Press.

Davie, G. (1994), *Religion in Britain since 1945.* Oxford: Basil Blackwell.

Graham, L. K. (1992), *Care of Persons, Care of Worlds.* Nashville: Abingdon.

Ross, A. (2003), *Counselling Skills for Church and Faith Community Workers.* Buckinghamshire: Open University Press.

Woodhead, L. and Heelas, P. (2000), *Religion in Modern Time: An Interpretive Anthology*. Oxford: Basil Blackwell.

4   Care across the Life-course

Bentall, R. P. (2003), *Madness Explained: Psychosis Explained*. London: Allen Lane/Penguin.

Davey, B. (ed.) (2001), *Birth to Old Age: Health in Transition*. Buckinghamshire: Open University Press.

Ford, N. M. (2002), *The Prenatal Person*. Oxford: Basil Blackwell.

HMSO (2003), *UK 2004: The Official Yearbook of the United Kingdom of Great Britain and Northern Ireland*. London: TSO.

Jewell, A. (2003), *Ageing, Spirituality and Wellbeing*. London: Jessica Kingsley.

Lynch, G. (2002), *Pastoral Care & Counselling*. London: Sage.

Shamy, E. (2003), *A Guide to the Spiritual Dimension of Care for People with Alzheimer's Disease and Related Dementia*. London: Jessica Kingsley.

Swinton, J. (2000), *Resurrecting the Person: Friendship and the Care of People with Mental Health Problems*. Nashville: Abingdon.

WHO (2004), *Promoting Mental Health: Concepts, Emerging Evidence, Practice*. Geneva: World Health Organization.

5   The Care and Support of Bereaved People

Attig, T. (1996) *How We Grieve: Relearning the World*. New York: Oxford University Press.

Bonanno, G. A. and Kaltman, S. (2001), 'The Varieties of Grief Experience', *Clinical Psychology Review*, vol. 21, no. 5, pp. 705–34.

Department of Health (2005), *When a Patient Dies: Advice on Developing Bereavement Services in the NHS*. London: Department of Health (Consultation Document).

Gray, D. (2002), *Memorial Services*. London: SPCK.

Hockey, J., Katz, J. and Small, N. (2001), *Grief, Mourning and Death Ritual*. Buckinghamshire: Open University Press.

Lloyd-Williams, M. (ed.) (2003), *Psychosocial Issues in Palliative Care*. Oxford: Oxford University Press.

Neimeyer, R. A. and Anderson, A. (2001), 'Meaning Reconstruction Theory', in Thompson, N. (ed.), *Loss and Grief: A Guide for Human Services Practitioners*. Basingstoke: Palgrave.

Rees, D. (2001), *Death and Bereavement: The Psychological, Religious and Cultural Interfaces*. London: Whurr.

Relf, M. (2004), 'Risk Assessment and Bereavement Service', in Payne, S., Seymour, J. and Ingleton, C. (eds), *Palliative Care Nursing*. Maidenhead: McGraw-Hill.

Walter, T. (1999), *On Bereavement: The Culture of Grief*. Buckinghamshire: Open University Press.

Worden, J. W. (1996), *Children and Grief: When a Parent Dies*. New York: Guilford Press.

Worden, J. W. (2003), *Grief Counselling and Grief Therapy*. London: Brunner-Routledge (3rd edition).

6   Different Faiths, Ethnicity and Culture

Anderson, R. G. and Fukuyama, M. A. (eds) (2004), *Ministry in the Spiritual and Cultural Diversity of Health Care*. New York: Haworth Press.

Davie, G. (1994), *Religion in Britain since 1945*. Oxford: Basil Blackwell.

Davie, G. (2002), *Europe: The Exceptional Case*. London: DLT.

Gilliat-Ray, S. (2001), 'Sociological Perspectives on the Pastoral Care of Minority Faiths in Hospital', in Orchard, H. (ed.), *Spirituality in Health Care Contexts*. London: Jessica Kingsley.

Lartey, E. Y. (2003), *In Living Color*. London: Jessica Kingsley (2nd edition).

ONS (2004), *Focus on Religion*. London: Office for National Statistics.

7 Non-clinical Work

Department of Health (2005), *Standards for Better Health*. London: Department of Health.

Mowat, H., Swinton, J., Guest, C. and Grant, L. (2005), *What Do Chaplains Do? The Role of the Chaplain in Meeting the Spiritual Needs of Patients*. Aberdeen: Mowat Research.

National Institute for Clinical Excellence (2002), *Principles for Best Practice in Clinical Audit*. Abingdon: Radcliffe Medical Press.

NHS (2003), *NHS Leadership Qualities Framework*. London: Department of Health/NHS Leadership Centre.

Volunteering England (www.volunteering.org.uk).

West, M. (1994), *Effective Teamwork*. London: BPS Books.

8 Professional Practice

Cobb, M. (2001), 'Walking on Water? The Moral Foundations of Chaplaincy', in Orchard, H. (ed.), *Spirituality in Health Care Contexts*. London: Jessica Kingsley.

Department of Health (2003), *Confidentiality: NHS Code of Practice*. London: Department of Health.

Department of Health (2005), *Records Management: NHS Code of Practice*. London: Department of Health.

Lynch, G. (1999), *Clinical Counselling in Pastoral Settings*. London: Routledge.

Lynch, G. (2002), *Pastoral Care & Counselling*. London: Sage.

9   Ritual and Liturgy

Bell, J. L. and Maule, G. (1997), *When Grief is Raw*. Glasgow: Wild Goose Publications.

Burgess, R. (ed.) (2001), *A Book of Blessings: And How to Write Your Own*. Glasgow: Wild Goose Publications.

Cretney, S. M. (2000), *Family Law*. London: Sweet & Maxwell.

Dudley, M. (1997), *A Manual for Ministry to the Sick*. London: SPCK.

Faculty Office (1992 and 1999), *Anglican Marriages in England and Wales: A Guide to the Law for Clergy*. London: The Faculty Office.

Green, R. (1988), *Only Connect: Worship and Liturgy from the Perspective of Pastoral Care*. London: DLT.

Horton, R. A. (2000), *Using Common Worship: Funerals*. London: Church House Publishing.

Perham, M. (2000), *New Handbook of Pastoral Liturgy*. London: SPCK.

Registrar General (1997), *Suggestions for the Guidance of the Clergy with Reference to the Marriage and Registration Act etc*. London: Office for National Statistics (www.statistics.gov.uk).

Stuart, E. (1992), *Daring to Speak Love's Name: A Gay and Lesbian Prayer Book*. London: Hamish Hamilton.

Ward, H. and Wild, J. (eds) (1995), *Human Rites: Worship Resources for An Age of Change*. London: Mowbray.

12   Code of Conduct

AHPCC, CHCC and SACH (2005), *Health Care Chaplains Code of Conduct*. Association of Hospice and Palliative Care Chaplains, College of Health Care Chaplains, Scottish Association of Chaplains in Healthcare.

Appendix   Services to Accompany Chapter 9: Ritual and Liturgy

Bell, J. L. and Maule, G. (1997), *When Grief Is Raw*. Glasgow: Wild Goose Publications.

Burgess, R. (ed.) (2001), *A Book of Blessings: And How to Write Your Own*. Glasgow: Wild Goose Publications.

Church of the Province of New Zealand (1989), *A New Zealand Prayer Book – He Karakia Mihinare o Aotearoa*. Auckland: Collins.

Church of the Province of Southern Africa (1989), *An Anglican Prayer Book 1989*. London: Collins.

Church of Scotland (1994), *Book of Common Order of the Church of Scotland*. Edinburgh: St Andrew Press.

Cotter, J. (1990), *Healing – More or Less*. Sheffield: Cairns Publications.

Morley, J. (1992), *All Desires Known*. London: SPCK.

The Archbishops' Council (2000), *Common Worship: Services and Prayers for the Church of England*. London: Church House Publishing.

The Archbishops' Council (2000), *Common Worship: Pastoral Services*. London: Church House Publishing.

The Uniting Church in Australia Assembly Commission on Liturgy (2005), *Uniting in Worship 2.* Sydney: The Assembly of the Uniting Churches in Australia.

Journals

Contact: The Interdisciplinary Journal of Pastoral Studies. Contact Pastoral Trust, UK.

Journal of Health Care Chaplaincy. The Haworth Press, USA.

Journal of Health Care Chaplains. College of Health Care Chaplains, UK.

Journal of Pastoral Care and Counseling. The Journal of Pastoral Care Publications, USA.

Scottish Journal of Healthcare Chaplaincy. Scottish Association of Chaplains in Healthcare, UK.

11

Resources and Organizations

Chaplaincy-related organizations

Association of Hospice and Palliative Care Chaplains (AHPCC)
www.ahpcc.org.uk

The Association exists to promote good standards among chaplains involved in the pastoral and spiritual care of people (including carers) facing death from a life-threatening illness. AHPCC aims to identify and promote good practice, be an agent of professional development, provide professional support and fellowship, and promote links with relevant church bodies and faith communities. The Association publishes a newsletter and runs regional groups. It also publishes a set of standards for hospice and palliative care chaplains and promotes a set of competencies for spiritual and religious care in specialist palliative care in association with Marie Curie.

Chaplaincy Academic and Accreditation Board (CAAB)
www.caabweb.org.uk

The CAAB is an advisory board to the professional bodies of chaplaincy in the UK and exists to develop the highest academic standards relating to the training and practice of healthcare chaplains and to promote the theory and knowledge of chaplaincy. The Board makes recommendations concerning professional education and training for chaplains at all levels and operates a scheme for awarding points in recognition of continuing professional education.

The Board derives its authority from the professional associations that recognize it and to whom it is accountable: the Association of Hospice and Palliative Care Chaplains (AHPCC), the College of Health Care Chaplaincy (CHCC) and the Scottish Association of Chaplains in Healthcare (SACH). In addition, the Board is quality assured through an Academic Reference Panel that provides academic peer review and advice.

College of Health Care Chaplaincy (CHCC)
www.healthcarechaplains.org

The CHCC is a professional association of chaplains that exists to promote the professional standing of healthcare chaplaincy and that of its members. It fulfils this through representing the profession on matters affecting chaplaincy in healthcare, providing professional development and educational opportunities, maintaining high standards of chaplaincy practice through a Code of Conduct, and supporting chaplains through a system of regional branches that organize meetings and activities for local members.

The College is a UK-wide organization that represents healthcare chaplains working in the NHS, private and voluntary sectors. It maintains a voluntary register of chaplains and provides professional indemnity insurance cover to its members. It also fulfils the functions of a trade union for its members as an autonomous professional section of Amicus. This ensures representation at work for individual members and representation for the chaplaincy profession at a national level as the staff negotiating body for terms and conditions of chaplains employed in the NHS. The College is accountable to its members and operates within the rules of Amicus.

European Network of Health Care Chaplaincy
www.eurochaplains.org

A network consisting of representatives from churches, faiths and national chaplaincy associations to enable its participants to share and learn from one another, to work for the development of professional guidelines and to promote a high-quality standard of healthcare chaplaincy in Europe. The network holds biennial consultations and hosts a website with European-wide links and resources.

Faith Communities
www.churches-together.org.uk/whatwedo_healthcare_
 chaplaincy.html
www.jvisit.org.uk/hospital
www.nhs-chaplaincy-spiritualcare.org.uk

The faith communities are constituted by religious populations and represented by a range of organizations at both a local and national level. The main faith community is Christianity, which has three denominational bodies that deal with chaplaincy matters: the Hospital Chaplaincies Council for the Church of England, the Health Care Chaplaincy Steering Committee for the Free Churches Group of Churches Together in England, and the Catholic Health Advisers and Episcopal Representative for the Roman Catholic Bishops' Conference of England and Wales. These bodies act in an advisory capacity to their denominations and support chaplains by providing advice, guidance and training opportunities. In addition, the Hospital Chaplaincies Council co-ordinates the Assessors' Panel for the appointment of chaplains.

One in twenty of the population belong to other faith communities, of which the largest populations are Muslim, Hindu, Sikh, Jewish and Buddhist. There are currently no national bodies that deal with chaplaincy matters in these faith communities. However, some faith communities have national committees and groups that deal with health and medical matters – for example, the Health and Medical Committee of the Muslim Council of Britain – and some have local bodies that deal with pastoral care – for example, the Hospital Visitation Committee of the United Synagogue of London.

Healthcare Chaplaincy Training and Development Unit for Scotland
www.chaplains.co.uk

The Unit is part of NHS Education for Scotland (NES) and provides training opportunities and develops educational opportunities for chaplains. It assists the Scottish NHS Boards in the development and implementation of Spiritual Care Policies and liaises with faith communities, churches and minority groups to facilitate their relationship with NHS Scotland. In addition, the Unit aims to monitor and ensure an adequate system of support and supervision for chaplains as well as share information, good practice and developments with chaplaincy professional organizations in Scotland, the UK and elsewhere.

Multi-Faith Group for Healthcare Chaplaincy (MFGHC)
www.mfghc.com

The MFGHC is a membership organization that exists to advance multi-faith healthcare chaplaincy in England and Wales. It aims to provide a means of consultation between the faith communities and to work in co-operation with health-care and chaplaincy organizations. In particular, the MFGHC seeks to develop agreed standards across all faith groups and within healthcare organizations, to develop a system of asses-sors for appointment interviews currently undertaken by the Panel of Assessors and to promote the education and training of healthcare chaplains. Full membership of the MFGHC is open to faith groups in the UK, and also to chaplaincy bodies that are multi-faith in their purpose, membership and gover-nance. The work of the Group is reported to constituent organizations.

Scottish Association of Chaplains in Healthcare (SACH)
www.sach.org.uk

SACH is a professional body representing the interests of chaplains in healthcare in Scotland. The Association provides a range of benefits to its members that include an online newsletter, journal, training opportunities, and professional and indemnity insurance. SACH aims to promote, set and maintain high standards of chaplaincy and provide a Code of Practice to further them, give support and fellowship, and promote theological reflection. The Association also aims to establish and promote good working relationships with religious and other organizations concerned with the promotion of healthcare and to keep and publish a register of members.

Other organizations

Higher Education Institutions (HEIs)
Higher education provides the educational entry route for most health professions and it is part of lifelong learning. Higher educational programmes for health professionals are delivered by universities and colleges (HEIs) who have their own powers to award qualifications from certificate to doctoral level. HEIs also conduct and provide opportunities for research, which is fundamental to the development of the knowledge, understanding and practice of healthcare. The educational entry level for most health professions is an honours degree and, in general, HEIs are responsible for ensuring that students meet the requirements for professional competency and therefore recommend entry onto a professional register. In some professions people may only practise if, in addition to completing a degree course, they pass the examinations of their professional body.

Universities are self-governing and legally independent organizations. They operate either under a royal charter or under an Instrument of Government and Articles of Government. Academic standards and quality in higher education are subject to a peer review process undertaken by the Quality Assurance Agency (QAA) and the quality of research is rated through a national Research Assessment Exercise (RAE).

Regulatory bodies

The regulatory bodies for health professions exist to create and maintain high standards of competence and conduct and, when necessary, to protect the public. Regulators provide four main functions: setting standards of conduct and practice for their professions; setting and promoting high standards of education; maintaining a list of properly qualified professionals (a register); and dealing with professionals whose fitness to practise is in doubt.

Professional bodies can be regulators: for example, the Royal Pharmaceutical Society of Great Britain (RPSGB) is the regulatory and professional body for pharmacists whose primary objective is to lead, regulate and develop the pharmacy profession. The functions of advancing the interests of the health professionals and regulating them can be separate: for example, the professional association for dietitians is the British Dietetic Association (BDA) and their regulator body is the Health Professions Council (HPC). The HPC is independent of the NHS and is run by an elected Council made up of members of the professions regulated, plus members of the public. It currently regulates 13 healthcare professions but is able to take on the regulation of further professions. If NHS chaplaincy were to be subject to statutory regulation, then it is likely that the HPC would be the regulatory body.

Workforce Development Confederations & Directorates (WDCs & WDDs)
www.nationalworkforce.nhs.uk
www.sywdc.nhs.uk

Workforce Development organizations plan and develop the healthcare workforce to meet the needs of the service and professional requirements for Strategic Health Authorities. They work with local employers, professional groups, Higher Education Institutions and other organizations to ensure the delivery of adequate numbers of properly trained staff, and the growth and development of the NHS workforce within a framework of lifelong learning. They are responsible for commissioning and managing quality-assured education and training for all staff supported through the Multi-Professional Education and Training budget and other central Department of Health budgets in accordance with national commitments and local plans. Workforce Development organizations are usually a directorate within a Strategic Health Authority.

As the lead Workforce Development organization for chaplaincy in the NHS in England, the South Yorkshire WDC is responsible for the development and implementation of a national strategy for the chaplaincy and spiritual healthcare workforce that includes proposals for an expanded career map and a new educational framework. The implementation of the strategy is supported by four lead chaplains funded through the English Workforce Development organizations and managed by South Yorkshire WDC.

Chaplaincy-related resources

Hospital Chaplaincy Gateway
www.hospitalchaplain.com

This site provides a wide range of resources for hospital chaplains in pastoral care, spiritual care, religious care and general healthcare chaplaincy. There are articles and documents as well as links to other sites and departments around the world.

JISCmail
www.jiscmail.ac.uk/lists/chaplaincy-spirituality-health.html

JISCmail is a mailing list service for the higher education, further education and research communities. It supports discussion, collaboration and communication by e-mail or via the web. The chaplaincy-spirituality-health list provides a network for chaplains, educationalists and researchers.

NMAP
http://nmap.ac.uk

The Nursing, Midwifery and Allied Health Professions is a gateway to evaluated, quality internet resources, aimed at students, researchers, academics and practitioners in the health and medical sciences. NMAP is created by a core team of information specialists and subject experts co-ordinated at the University of Nottingham Greenfield Medical Library, in partnership with key organizations throughout the UK.

Content providers from relevant professional organizations help to ensure that NMAP meets the needs of the professions. It is closely integrated with the OMNI gateway.

National electronic Library for Health (NeLH)
http://www.nelh.nhs.uk

The NeLH is a resource to help the NHS achieve its objectives by complementing and supplementing NHS libraries. Its collection focuses on the new types of quality-assured knowledge produced by organizations such as the Cochrane Collaboration and the Centre for Reviews and Dissemination. Part of the content has restricted access and users will need to register for an Athens password.

Websites

Bahai Community of the UK
www.bahai.org.uk

Board of Deputies of British Jews
www.bod.org.uk

Adherents.com
www.adherents.com

BBC Religion and Ethics
www.bbc.co.uk/religion

Buddha Net
www.buddhanet.net

Centre for the Study of Islam and Christian–Muslim Relations
www.theology.bham.ac.uk/postgrad/islam/news.htm

Chief Rabbi (The)
www.chiefrabbi.org

Churches' Commission for Racial Justice
www.ccrj.org.uk

Council of Christian and Jews
www.ccj.org.uk

Ethnicity online – cultural awareness in healthcare
www.ethnicityonline.net

Forum Against Islamophobia and Racism (FAIR)
www.fairuk.org/intro.htm

Hindu Universe
www.hindunet.org

Institute for Jewish Policy Research
www.jpr.org.uk

Inter Faith Network
www.interfaith.org.uk

Islamic Affairs Central Network
www.iacn.org.uk

Jewish Council for Racial Equality
www.jcore.org.uk

Multi Faith Net
www.multifaithnet.org

Muslim Council for Britain
www.mcb.org.uk

National Secular Society
www.secularism.org.uk

Sikhnet
www.sikhnet.com

Three Faiths Forum
www.threefaithsforum.org.uk

12

Code of Conduct

The Association of Hospice and Palliative Care Chaplains, the College of Health Care Chaplains and the Scottish Association of Chaplains in Healthcare publish a joint Code of Conduct that sets out the professional standards expected of chaplains. This chapter contains the core elements of the Code. The full Code is available from the professional associations. The Code complements the policies and rules of employing health bodies, which apply to all staff, and normally cover issues such as absence, timekeeping and holiday arrangements, health and safety, discrimination, bullying and harassment.

General conduct of chaplains

Healthcare chaplains are responsible for their personal and professional conduct and must be able to justify their actions and practice to those in their care and to colleagues. In particular chaplains must:

- act at all times in ways that promote trust and confidence in their profession;
- act at all times to promote and safeguard the interests and well-being of those in their care;
- affirm the equal dignity and worth of those in their care;
- act with integrity and with due respect for diversity and differences including, but not limited to, ethnicity, gender, sexual orientation, age, disability, religion and spirituality;
- respect the right of each faith group to hold their own values, traditions, beliefs and practices;

- maintain good standing in their own faith community if appointed on that basis;
- ensure that their conduct, dress and personal appearance is consistent with their profession and appropriate to the setting in which they work.

Relationships between chaplains and those in their care

Relationships established by chaplains with those in their care have the capacity to be nurturing and healing, but they also have the potential to be damaging and destructive. An important reason for this is the intrinsic imbalance of power in the relationship. Chaplains must therefore exercise their power with sensitivity, discernment and within ethical boundaries. The only appropriate relationship between chaplains and those in their care is a professional relationship committed to promote the spiritual good and best interests of particular individuals. Moving the focus away from meeting the needs of those in their care towards meeting the chaplain's own needs is unprofessional and an abuse of power.

Maintaining trust

Spiritual care is both a privilege and a responsibility and chaplains need to establish boundaries that enable trust and safeguard ethical relationships with those in their care. In particular chaplains must:

- behave in ways that honour the dignity and value of those in their care;
- ensure that no action or omission on their part and within their sphere of responsibility could be detrimental to the well-being of those in their care;
- understand the limits of professional discretion and respect the trust established with those in their care;
- respect the autonomy of those in their care including the freedom to make decisions contrary to the beliefs, practices or opinions of the chaplain;

- recognize and act within the limits of their competence;
- maintain clear boundaries in the areas of self-disclosure, intimacy and sexuality;
- avoid any conflicts of interest but in the event that a chaplain has to withdraw on the grounds of conscience, faith or ethical principles, endeavour to refer to another chaplain and facilitate the transfer and continuity of care.

Respecting confidentiality

Confidentiality is an expression of trust that enables vulnerable people to seek help from strangers at a time of need and to talk about personal, private and secret matters relevant to their spiritual health and well-being. Spiritual care cannot be provided without access to confidential information. Chaplains must therefore respect and promote confidences, and in particular they must:

- respect the right of individuals to control access to their own personal information and to limit its disclosure;
- establish the boundaries of confidentiality with those in their care and respect as far as possible the limitations of disclosure that an individual can reasonably expect or request;
- treat information about those in their care as confidential and use it only for the purposes for which it was given;
- guard against breaches of confidentiality by protecting information from improper disclosure at all times;
- ensure that confidential information is not disclosed to a third party unless there are clear grounds for disclosure including: (1) the consent of the individual; (2) the public interest, particularly where there is a risk of harm; (3) and in accordance with an order of a court or other public body that has jurisdiction;[1]

---

1 DoH (2003) *Confidentiality: NHS Code of Conduct*. London: Department of Health.

- discuss with those in their care reasons why disclosing confidential information to other chaplains or members of the healthcare team may be beneficial to providing good care;
- only disclose confidential information about those in their care who are not capable of consent (for example, because they are unconscious) on the grounds of necessity if it is clearly in the individual's interest and the disclosure is not contrary to the individual's known values and beliefs;
- uphold the absolute confidentiality of information disclosed within a formal act of confession that has been requested by the individual and takes place in certain faith traditions under a mutually understood 'seal of the confessional'.[2]

Abuse

Abuse is a violation of an individual's human and civil rights by any other person or persons.[3] It is behaviour that is a clear breach of the ethical conduct required of chaplains. It can result from a misuse of power or a betrayal of trust, respect or intimacy which causes harm or exploitation. It can be caused by purposeful or negligent actions as well as a failure to act where a duty exists. The main forms of abuse include spiritual, physical, psychological, verbal, sexual, and financial:

- spiritual abuse is the imposition of a chaplain's values and beliefs on those in their care, proselytism or a failure to respect their spiritual interests;

---

2 Convocations of Canterbury and York (2003) *Guidelines for the Professional Conduct of the Clergy*. London: Church House Publishing. Section 7.

Cardinal Secretary of State (1983) *The Code of Canon Law*. London: Collins. Canon 983.

3 DoH (2000) *No secrets: Guidance on developing and implementing multi-agency policies and procedures to protect vulnerable adults from abuse*. London: Department of Health. Section 2.

- physical abuse is any form of physical contact or neglect which is likely to cause distress, pain or bodily harm;
- psychological abuse is behaviour by a chaplain which is exploitative, manipulative, coercive or intimidating;
- verbal abuse is spoken remarks by a chaplain which are disrespectful, humiliating, intimidating or harmful to those in a chaplain's care;
- sexual abuse is forcing, coercing or inducing any person in the care of the chaplain to establish or pursue a sexual or improper emotional relationship.
- financial or material abuse is the misappropriation of a person's money or assets by a chaplain through fraud or deception; or a chaplain's misuse of a person's assets or money while having a legitimate access to them.[4]

The use of touch

Touch is a basic human gesture and physical contact is an integral part of healthcare. Touch conveys to many people reassurance, care and concern and it can be a valuable expression of a supportive or therapeutic relationship. But touch is not value-free, it is conditioned by social and cultural norms and it can convey powerful signals. Therefore touch may be perceived as threatening or manipulative, it could be physically painful and it can be a form of abuse. In the healthcare context the use of touch must also be evaluated in relationship to hand hygiene and precautions required for infection control.

Chaplains use touch informally as a gesture of care and formally within rituals to signify beliefs and theological actions. However, because the use of touch can be misunderstood or misinterpreted, or it may be unwanted, particular sensitivity should be exercised and assumptions about gender

---

4 Chaplains must comply with the financial instructions of their employing health body regarding the handling of money received from public acts of worship or gifts of money towards hospital chapels or trust funds.

and personal space carefully considered. If in any doubt as
to whether touch may be acceptable, permission should be
obtained. The use of ritual that involves touch should be carefully explained and permission obtained. Where an individual
does not have the capacity to consent, a chaplain may act on
the grounds of necessity if it is clearly in the individual's interest and it is not contrary to the individual's known values and
beliefs; or, in the case of a minor lacking capacity, is not contrary to the wishes of someone with parental responsibility.

Working with colleagues

Providing spiritual care cannot be accomplished by working
in isolation and chaplains must be able to work effectively
with other chaplains, health and social care professionals,
ministers of religion and representatives of faith groups or
communities. In particular chaplains must:

- respect the skills, contributions and integrity of colleagues;
- work in a collaborative and co-operative manner with
  colleagues and communicate effectively with them within
  the limits of confidentiality;
- participate in the work of multidisciplinary teams they are
  members of and respect their confidentiality;[5]
- ensure there is a formal handover of continuing care of
  patients to another colleague at the end of a shift or com-
  mencement of leave;
- work within professional protocols when receiving or initiating referrals and liaising with colleagues outside of the
  employing health body;
- challenge colleagues who appear to have behaved unethi-
  cally or in contravention of this Code. In addition be

---

5 AHPCC (2003) *Standards for Hospice and Palliative Care Chap-
laincy.* Association of Hospice and Palliative Care Chaplains. Standard
No. 3. NHS QIS (2002) *Clinical Standards.* Edinburgh: NHS Quality
Improvement Scotland. Standards 3a and 3b.

prepared to bring concerns of misconduct to those charged with responsibility for colleagues.

Probity in professional practice

The office of a chaplain requires the highest standards of moral integrity and honesty. In particular chaplains must:

- be honest and accurate in representing their professional affiliations, qualifications and experience, and not make unjustifiable claims about their competence;
- distinguish between pastoral care and formal counselling and ensure that those in their care understand the form of support being offered;
- refrain from encouraging those in their care to give, lend or bequeath money or gifts which will be of a direct or indirect benefit, or put pressure on those in their care to make donations;
- manage any finances for which they are responsible with diligence and for the purpose for which they are intended;
- declare any commercial involvement that might cause a conflict of interest;
- only conduct or participate in research that fulfils the requirements of research governance;
- demonstrate honesty and objectivity when providing references for colleagues or completing and signing forms. Chaplains must take reasonable steps to verify any statement before they sign a document, and they must not write or sign documents which are false or misleading.

Appendix

Services to Accompany Chapter 9:
Ritual and Liturgy

**A Service for Blessing a Memorial Window – see pages
124–5**

Gracious God,
you hold all souls in life,
and bind together all your people
in heaven and on earth.
We thank you for those who have been lights in the world
in whose lives we have seen reflections of your goodness and
    love.

Today we thank you for N
whose life and work we commemorate;
for her vocation to nurse the sick
for her inspiration to others
and for the beautiful and good in her life which brightened
    the lives of others.

In the name of God
and in the memory of N
we dedicate and bless this window
that it may be a source of joy and hope
and lighten the hearts of all those
who pass by this place.

May God, the source of all light
help us to walk
without stumbling in the path of life;
illumine our way
and lead us into glory. Amen.

A Service of Baptism for a Baby Who Is Critically Ill or Injured – see pages 125–7

Words of welcome and introduction may be used

In baptism God calls us to be his friends
and to make us holy in his Son Jesus Christ.

Prayer over the water

We thank you, almighty God, for the gift of water
to sustain, refresh and cleanse all life.
Over water the Holy Spirit moved in the beginning of
   creation.
Through water you led the children of Israel
from slavery in Egypt to freedom in the promised land.
In water your Son Jesus received the baptism of John
and was anointed by the Holy Spirit to proclaim your
   redeeming love.[1]
Now bless this water,
that those who are washed in it
may be made one with Christ
in the fellowship of your Church,
and be brought through every tribulation
to share the risen life
that is ours in Jesus Christ our Lord. Amen.[2]

The Baptism

To the parents:
What name have you given this child?
The parents respond with the Christian name(s) of the child:

Is it your wish that N is baptized?

---

1 Baptism, *Common Worship*, p. 364.
2 Emergency Baptism, *Common Worship: Pastoral Services*, p. 195
(adapted).

To godparents and supporters (if present):
Is it your intention to support N with your prayers and love?

N,
for you Jesus Christ came into the world;
for you he lived and showed God's love;
[for you he suffered death on the Cross;
for you he triumphed over death,
rising to newness of life:]
for you he prays at God's right hand:
    all this for you,
        before you could know anything of it.
In your Baptism,
the word of Scripture is fulfilled:
'We love, because God first loved us.'[3]

The Baptism

N, I baptize you
in the name of the Father,
and of the Son,
and of the Holy Spirit.
Amen.

Signing with the Cross

May God, who has received you by baptism into his Church,
pour upon you the riches of his grace,
that within the company of Christ's pilgrim people
you may be renewed by his anointing Spirit,
and come to the inheritance of the saints in glory. Amen.[4]

---

3 *Uniting in Worship* 2 (adapted).
4 Baptism, *Common Worship*, p. 337.

Prayers of Intercession for the Family

Eternal God, our beginning and our end,
preserve in your people the new life of baptism;
as Christ receives us on earth,
so may he guide us through the trials of this world,
and enfold us in the joy of heaven,
where you live and reign,
one God for ever and ever. Amen.[5]

The Lord's Prayer

Our Father, who art in heaven,
hallowed be thy name;
thy kingdom come;
thy will be done;
on earth as it is in heaven.
Give us this day our daily bread.
And forgive us our trespasses,
as we forgive those who trespass against us.
And lead us not into temptation;
but deliver us from evil.
For thine is the kingdom,
the power and the glory,
for ever and ever.
Amen.

The Blessing

May God give to you and to those you love
his comfort and his peace,
and the blessing of God,
the Father, the Son and the Holy Spirit,
rest upon you this day and for evermore.
Amen.

---

5 Baptism, *Common Worship*, p. 362.

A Service for Confession and Reconciliation[6] – see pages 127–8

The Welcome

May the grace of the Holy Spirit fill your heart with light, that you may confess your sins with loving trust, and come to know that God is merciful.

Reading of Scripture

A suitable passage may be read and discussed, for example: Psalm 130; Luke 15.1–9; John 20.19–23; 1 Corinthians 13.4–7

The Confession

The penitent makes her or his confession in these or similar words
Most merciful God, have mercy upon me. In your compassion forgive my sins both known and unknown, things done and left undone (especially . . .). O God, uphold me by your Spirit, that I may live and serve you in newness of life to the honour and glory of your Name, through Jesus Christ our Lord. Amen

Spiritual Guidance

The priest may offer prayer on behalf of the penitent, and give advice if judged appropriate. Prayer or some other action may be suggested as a token of repentance and thanksgiving.

The Absolution

God, the Father of mercies, through the death and resurrection of his Son has reconciled the world to himself and forgives all who repent and believe in him. Through his ministry of reconciliation and by his authority committed to me you

---

6 Rite 2, *An Anglican Prayer Book 1989* (Church of the Province of Southern Africa), pp. 451–3.

are absolved from all your sins: in the name of the Father, and of the Son, and of the Holy Spirit. Amen.

A prayer for healing with the laying on of hands may follow. In special circumstances the penitent may be anointed.

The Conclusion

Christ our friend,
you ask for our love
in spite of our betrayal.
Give us courage to embrace forgiveness,
know you again,
and trust ourselves in you,
Amen.[7]

Blessing

A Prayer of Reconciliation

Intimate God,
you are able to accept in us
what we cannot even acknowledge;
you have named in us
what we cannot bear to speak of;
you hold in your memory
what we have tried to forget;
you will hold out to us
a glory we cannot imagine.
Reconcile us through your cross
to all that we have rejected in ourselves,
that we may find no part of your creation
to be alien or strange to us,
and that we ourselves may be made whole,
through Jesus Christ, our lover and our friend.
Amen.[8]

---

7 Janet Morley, *All Desires Known.*
8 Janet Morley, *All Desires Known.*

A Service for the Laying on of Hands and Anointing the Sick – see pages 128–9

N, may the Holy Spirit,
the Giver of all life and healing,
fill you with Light and Love,
and make you whole;
through Jesus Christ our Saviour.[9]

Anointing

N, through faith in the power and the will
of our Saviour Jesus Christ
to make you whole and holy,
to consecrate you with joy
for ever deeper service and friendship,
to give you courage
to go through the narrow gates of your journey,
I anoint you with oil
in the name of God,
who gives you life,
bears your pain,
and makes you whole.
Amen.[10]

The Laying on of Hands and Anointing for a Dying Person[11]

In the name of our Lord Jesus Christ
I lay my hands on you, N.
May the Lord in his mercy and love uphold you
by the grace and power of the Holy Spirit.
May he deliver you from all evil,

---

9 Jim Cotter, *Healing – More or Less*, p. 66.
10 Jim Cotter, *Healing – More or Less*, p. 68.
11 Ministry at the Time of Death, *Common Worship: Pastoral Services*, p. 226.

give you light and peace,
and bring you to everlasting life.
Amen.

The Anointing of a Dying Person

N, I anoint you with oil in the name of our Lord Jesus Christ.
May the Lord in his love and mercy uphold you
by the grace and power of the Holy Spirit.
Amen.

The minister says

As you are outwardly anointed with this holy oil,
so may our heavenly Father grant you the inward anointing
    of the Holy Spirit.
Of his great mercy
may he forgive you your sins
and release you from suffering.
May he deliver you from all evil,
preserve you in all goodness
and bring you to everlasting life;
through Jesus Christ our Lord.
Amen.

A Service for Distribution of Holy Communion in Hospital[12] – see pages 129–31

The Greeting

The peace of the Lord be always with you.

Words of Introduction

The Church of God, of which we are members, has taken bread and wine and given thanks over them according to our Lord's command. These holy gifts are now offered to us that, with faith and thanksgiving, we may share in the communion of the body and blood of Christ.

Prayer of Preparation

Almighty God,
to whom all hearts are open,
all desires known,
and from whom no secrets are hidden:
cleanse the thoughts of our hearts
by the inspiration of your Holy Spirit,
that we may perfectly love you,
and worthily magnify your holy name;
through Christ our Lord.
Amen.

Prayers of Penitence

Come to me, all who labour and are heavy laden,
and I will give you rest.

---

12 Distribution of Holy Communion, *Common Worship: Pastoral Services*, pp. 80–5.

God shows his love for us
in that while we were still sinners, Christ died for us.
Let us then show our love for him
by confessing our sins in penitence and faith.

**Almighty God, our heavenly Father,
we have sinned against you
and against our neighbour
in thought and word and deed,
through negligence, through weakness,
through our own deliberate fault.
We are truly sorry
and repent of all our sins.
For the sake of your Son Jesus Christ,
who died for us,
forgive us all that is past,
and grant that we may serve you in newness of life
to the glory of your name.
Amen.**

Almighty God,
who forgives all who truly repent,
have mercy upon us,
pardon and deliver us from all our sins,
confirm and strengthen us in all goodness,
and keep us in life eternal;
through Jesus Christ our Lord.
Amen.

The Collect, Reading(s) and Prayers of Intercession

**The Laying on of Hands with Prayer and Anointing may
follow (see pages 168–9)**

The Lord's Prayer

Let us pray with confidence as our Saviour has taught us:

Our Father, who art in heaven,
hallowed be thy name;
thy kingdom come;
thy will be done;
on earth as it is in heaven.
Give us this day our daily bread.
And forgive us our trespasses,
as we forgive those who trespass against us.
And lead us not into temptation;
but deliver us from evil.
For thine is the kingdom,
the power and the glory,
for ever and ever.
Amen.

Giving of Communion

Jesus is the Lamb of God
who takes away the sin of the world.
Blessed are those who are called to his supper.
Lord, I am not worthy to receive you,
but only say the word, and I shall be healed.

This prayer may be said before the distribution

We do not presume
to come to this your table, merciful Lord,
trusting in our own righteousness,
but in your manifold and great mercies.
We are not worthy
so much as to gather up the crumbs under your table.
But you are the same Lord
whose nature is always to have mercy.
Grant us, therefore, gracious Lord,

so to eat the flesh of your dear Son Jesus Christ
and to drink his blood,
that our sinful bodies may be made clean by his body
and our souls washed through his most precious blood,
and that we may evermore dwell in him and he in us.
Amen.

The minister and people receive communion.

Prayer after Communion

Almighty God,
we thank you for feeding us
with the body and blood of your Son Jesus Christ.
Through him we offer you our souls and bodies
to be a living sacrifice.
Strengthen us
in the power of your Spirit
to live and work
to your praise and glory.
Amen.

Conclusion

The minister says the Grace or a suitable blessing.

A Service for the Affirmation of a Relationship – see page 131–2

Loving God,
you have known us from the beginning
and have invited us to love you in loving one another.
In your presence we come together
to affirm and celebrate
the love between N and N.
Open our hearts to one another and to you,
embrace us in our frail and beautiful flesh
and meet us in those we welcome as companions on our
     journey.

A suitable passage may be read and an address given:

Ruth 1.16–17; 1 Samuel 18.1–4; John 15.12–17.

In the presence of God,
before those with us today,
and supported by those unable to be here now,
we give thanks for the relationship of love
between you, N and N.
And we affirm the gifts
that you have found in one another
and in which you, and those who know you, delight.

Each may exchange a symbol of the relationship

May these gifts
be a symbol of all that you are to one another
a token of what we celebrate this day
and a sign to the world of the uniqueness of your
     relationship.

Prayers may be said by those present

God of intimacy,
you surround us with friends and family
to cherish and to challenge.
May we so give and receive caring
in the details of our lives
that we also remain faithful
to your greater demands,
through Jesus Christ, Amen.[13]

Blessing

May God hold you as a lover
May she caress your broken places,
May she dust you with gentleness,
and may you live in the world
As a sign of her touch.[14]

Renewal of Marriage Vows[15]

The minister says to the couple(s)
I invite you now to recall the vows that you made at your
   wedding.

Husband and wife face each other and hold hands.

The husband says
I, N, took you, N, to be my wife;

The wife says
I, N, took you, N, to be my husband;

The couple say together
to have and to hold from that day forward,
for better, for worse, for richer, for poorer,

---

13 Janet Morley, *All Desires Known*.
14 Rosie Miles, in R. Burgess (ed.), *A Book of Blessings*, p. 142.
15 Thanksgiving for Marriage, *Common Worship: Pastoral Services*,
pp. 188–93 (adapted).

in sickness and in health, to love and to cherish,
till death us do part, according to God's holy law,
and this was our solemn vow.
Today, in the presence of our family and friends,
we affirm our continuing commitment to this vow.

The minister says to the congregation
Will you, the family and friends of N and N,
continue to support and uphold them
in their marriage now and in the years to come?
We will.

The Rings

*If a new ring (or new rings) is to be blessed, this prayer may
be used*

Heavenly Father, source of everlasting love,
revealed to us in Jesus Christ and poured into our hearts
    through your Holy Spirit;
that love which many waters cannot quench, neither the
    floods drown;
that love which is patient and kind, enduring all things
    without end;
by your blessing, let these rings be to N and N
symbols to remind them of the covenant made on their
    wedding day,
through your grace in the love of your Son
and in the power of your Spirit.
Amen.

If a ring (or rings) is to be given these words are used

I give you this ring
as a sign of our marriage.
With my body I honour you,
all that I am I give to you,
and all that I have I share with you,

within the love of God,
Father, Son, and Holy Spirit.

Or, if not, each may touch the wedding ring(s) with the words

I gave you this ring
as a sign of our marriage.
With my body I honour you,
all that I am I give to you,
and all that I have I share with you,
within the love of God,
Father, Son, and Holy Spirit.

Prayers

The minister or others may pray, using these or similar prayers

God the Father,
God the Son,
God the Holy Spirit,
bless, preserve and keep you;
the Lord mercifully grant you the riches of his grace
that you may please him both in body and soul,
and, living together in faith and love,
may receive the blessings of eternal life.
Amen.

The Lord's Prayer

The minister blesses the couple and those present, saying

God the Holy Trinity make you strong in faith and love,
defend you on every side, and guide you in truth and peace;
and the blessing of God almighty,
the Father, the Son, and the Holy Spirit,
be among you and remain with you always.
Amen.

A Service for Commendation at the End of Life – see pages 132–3

A Gathering Prayer[16]

Heavenly Father,
you have not made us for darkness and death,
but for life with you for ever.
Without you we have nothing to hope for;
with you we have nothing to fear.
Speak to us now your words of eternal life.
Lift us from anxiety and guilt
to the light and peace of your presence,
and set the glory of your love before us;
through Jesus Christ our Lord.
Amen.

A Prayer for Those Keeping a Vigil with a Dying Person[17]

Lord,
in weakness or in strength
we bear your image.
We pray for those we love
who now live in a land of shadows,
where the light of memory is dimmed,
where the familiar lies unknown,
where the beloved become as strangers.
Hold them in your everlasting arms,
and grant to those who care
a strength to serve,
a patience to persevere,
a love to last

---

16 Second Order for a Funeral Service, *Book of Common Order of the Church of Scotland*, p. 264.

17 Ministry at the Time of Death, *Common Worship: Pastoral Services*, p. 346.

and a peace that passes human understanding.
Hold us in your everlasting arms,
today and for all eternity;
through Jesus Christ our Lord.
Amen.

When Life Support is Withdrawn

God of compassion and love,
you have breathed into us the breath of life
and have given us the exercise of our minds and wills.
In our frailty we surrender all life to you from whom it came,
trusting in your gracious promises;
through Jesus Christ our Lord. Amen.

Prayers of Commendation

Gracious God,
nothing in death or life,
nothing in the world as it is,
nothing in the world as it shall be,
nothing in all creation
can separate us from your love.
Jesus commended his spirit into your hands at his last hour.
Into those same hands we now commend your servant, *N*,
that dying to the world and cleansed from sin,
death may be for *him/her* the gate to life
and to eternal fellowship with you;
through the same Jesus Christ our Lord.
Amen.[18]

O God who brought us to birth,
and in whose arms we die,
we entrust to your embrace

---

18 Ministry at the Time of Death, *Common Worship: Pastoral Services*,
p. 230.

our beloved *sister/brother*.
Give *her/him* release from *her/his* pain,
courage to meet the darkness,
and grace to let go into new life,
through Jesus Christ, Amen.[19]

A Prayer for Those Who Mourn

Father, the death of N brings an emptiness into our lives.
We are separated from *him/her*
and feel broken and disturbed.
Give us confidence that *he/she* is safe
and *his/her* life complete with you,
and bring us together at the last
to the wholeness and fullness of your presence in heaven,
where your saints and angels enjoy you for ever and ever.
Amen.[20]

---

19 Janet Morley, *All Desires Known.*
20 Funeral, *Common Worship: Pastoral Services,* p. 355.

A Service for Naming and Commendation of a Dead Baby
– see pages 133–4

Opening Prayer

God of all comfort,
in this time of grief and distress
we have come to tell you our sorrow,
to name and commend this precious child to you,
and to pray for peace.
Be with us now,
and bring us in our sorrow
the comfort for which our hearts cry out;
through Jesus Christ our Lord. Amen.

Reading

Isaiah 49.15–16a; Psalm 139.1–18; Matthew 18.1–5, 10–14.

The Naming

To the parents
What name do you give your child?

O child whom we have barely known we call you *N*.
Receive this name as a sign of your uniqueness to us and to
    God.
By this name you will be remembered.

Commendation

God of compassion
you called into being this fragile life,
and you brought us hope.
As we prepare to say farewell
so give us faith to entrust *her/him* to you.
Take *her/him* into your arms
and welcome *her/him* into your eternal home

where there is no sorrow, nor weeping, nor pain,
but the fullness of peace and life everlasting.

Prayer for the Parents

Loving God,
be with us as we face the mystery of life and death,
and be with these parents who have known the joy of life
    beginning,
and the desolation of losing that life;
renew them in hope, faith and love
as they bear their loss,
and help them to go on from here with courage and
    confidence
in your care and love. Amen.

A Cradling Song[21]

We cannot care for you the way we wanted,
or cradle you or listen for your cry;
but, separated as we are by silence,
love will not die.

We cannot watch you grow into childhood
and find a new uniqueness every day;
but special as you would have been among us,
you still will stay.

We cannot know the pain or the potential
which passing years would summon or reveal;
but for that true fulfilment Jesus promised
we hope and feel.

So through the mess of anger, grief and tiredness,
through tensions which are not yet reconciled,
we give to God the worship of our sorrow
and our dear child.

---

21 John L. Bell and Graham Maule, *When Grief Is Raw*, p. 90.

Lord, in your arms which cradle all creation
we rest and place our baby beyond death,
believing that [*she*] now, alive in heaven,
breathes with your breath.

Index